January–April 20

Day by Day with God

Rooting women's lives in the Bible

The Bible Reading Fellowship
15 The Chambers, Vineyard
Abingdon OX14 3FE
brf.org.uk

The Bible Reading Fellowship (BRF) is a Registered Charity (233280)

ISBN 978 0 85746 911 3
All rights reserved

This edition © 2019 The Bible Reading Fellowship
Cover image © Thinkstock

Distributed in Australia by:
MediaCom Education Inc, PO Box 610, Unley, SA 5061
Tel: 1 800 811 311 | admin@mediacom.org.au

Distributed in New Zealand by:
Scripture Union Wholesale, PO Box 760, Wellington
Tel: 04 385 0421 | suwholesale@clear.net.nz

Acknowledgements
Scripture quotations marked NIV are taken from The Holy Bible, New International Version (Anglicised edition) copyright © 1979, 1984, 2011 by Biblica. Used by permission of Hodder & Stoughton Publishers, a Hachette UK company. All rights reserved. 'NIV' is a registered trademark of Biblica. UK trademark number 1448790. • Scripture quotations marked NLT are taken from the Holy Bible, New Living Translation, copyright © 1996, 2004, 2007, 2013. Used by permission of Tyndale House Publishers, Inc., Carol Stream, Illinois 60188. All rights reserved. • Scripture quotations marked MSG are taken from *The Message*, copyright © 1993, 1994, 1995, 1996, 2000, 2001, 2002 by Eugene H. Peterson. Used by permission of NavPress. All rights reserved. Represented by Tyndale House Publishers, Inc. • Scripture quotations taken from the Amplified® Bible (AMP), Copyright © 2015 by The Lockman Foundation. Used by permission. Lockman.org. • Scripture quotations marked NCV are taken from the New Century Version®. Copyright © 2005 by Thomas Nelson. Used by permission. All rights reserved. • Scripture quotations marked NRSV are taken from The New Revised Standard Version of the Bible, Anglicised edition, copyright © 1989, 1995 by the Division of Christian Education of the National Council of the Churches of Christ in the United States of America. Used by permission. All rights reserved. • Scripture quotations marked GNT are taken from the Good News Bible published by The Bible Societies/HarperCollins Publishers Ltd, UK © American Bible Society 1966, 1971, 1976, 1992, used with permission.

Every effort has been made to trace and contact copyright owners for material used in this resource. We apologise for any inadvertent omissions or errors, and would ask those concerned to contact us so that full acknowledgement can be made in the future.

A catalogue record for this book is available from the British Library

Printed by Gutenberg Press, Tarxien, Malta

Day by Day with God

Edited by **Ali Herbert** and **Jill Rattle** January–April 2020

- 6 **Ezekiel: the glory of the Lord**
  Amy Boucher Pye — *1–11 January*

- 18 **A letter to the Romans**
  Christine Platt — *12–25 January*

- 33 **Rest**
  Jean Watson — *26 January–1 February*

- 41 **Galatians: set free indeed**
  Chine McDonald — *2–15 February*

- 56 **A window into the heart of God: Revelation 2 and 3**
  Rachel Turner — *16–29 February*

- 71 **Thirsty for God: Book 2 of the Psalms**
  Nell Goddard — *1–7 March*

- 79 **Visions and visitations**
  Sara Batts — *8–21 March*

- 94 **From the beginning: Genesis 1—11**
  Tracy Williamson — *22 March–4 April*

- 110 **Holy ground**
  Rosemary Green — *5–18 April*

- 125 **Elijah and Elisha: faithful messengers**
  Fiona Barnard — *19–30 April*

Writers in this issue

Amy Boucher Pye is a writer, speaker and retreat leader who runs the *Woman Alive* book club. She's the author of the award-winning *Finding Myself in Britain* (Authentic, 2015) and *The Living Cross* (BRF, 2016). **amyboucherpye.com**

Christine Platt lives in New Zealand and enjoys the freedom and opportunities that retirement brings. As well as encouraging mission in her church, she also teaches English to Chinese people locally and to young people in East Timor.

Jean Watson grew up as a missionary kid in China, and now lives in the UK. She has worked as a teacher, a writer for TV and radio, and a spiritual accompanist. She writes poetry and loves cryptic crosswords and codewords.

Chine McDonald is a writer and broadcaster and head of Media & PR at Christian Aid. She is a trustee of Christians Against Poverty, Greenbelt, the Church & Media Network and the Sophia Network. She is a regular presenter on BBC Radio 4's *Thought for the Day* and *Daily Service*.

Rachel Turner is the Parenting for Faith Pioneer at BRF. Over the past 15 years she has worked across a variety of denominations as a children's, youth and family life pastor. She is the author of five books. **parentingforfaith.org**

Nell Goddard is a writer at the London Institute for Contemporary Christianity and author of *Musings of a Clergy Child* (BRF, 2017).

Sara Batts was previously a specialist librarian and is now a priest in the Diocese of Chelmsford. She lives with a dog and hosts a cat.

Tracy Williamson lives in Kent, sharing a home with her friend and ministry partner Marilyn Baker and their two assistance dogs. Tracy has written several books, her latest being *The Father's Kiss* (Authentic, 2018).

Rosemary Green has written for BRF since 1992. She enjoyed many years of shared ministry with her husband, Michael. Her main ministry is among seniors in her own church in Abingdon.

Fiona Barnard is a TEFL/ESOL teacher and staff member of Friends International. She works with international students, encouraging local Christians to reach out in friendship and evangelism to make disciples. She is an Honorary Chaplain at the University of St Andrews, Scotland.

Jill Rattle and Ali Herbert write...

Happy New Year! May you know God's nearness as you walk through the coming days. Whether you are entering a new year with vision, excitement and energy, or whether you are feeling drained and weary, we pray that opening the scriptures each day in company with our contributors will inspire you to press on, knowing that Jesus is by your side on the good days, on the bad days and even in the middle of the storm.

This issue beginning 2020 contains a lot about visions, visitations and encounters with God. (You'll read twice about Balaam's visitation, as we'd forgotten he appears in Revelation as well as Numbers!)

Jill has a sister who lives in a care home for people with a range of disabilities: her faith in Jesus shines strongly. One day, shortly after she lost her mother, she confided she had had a vision of Jesus. After describing the experience, she added, alight with wonder, 'But, Jill, you should have seen the look on his face!' Ah yes, if only...

Most of us will not have such vivid visions or visitations of God as those experienced by many we read about in the scriptures, but as we come and immerse ourselves day by day in his living word, as we open our hearts and minds in prayer and praise, we will see more of his glory, grace, forgiveness, compassion, kindness, faithfulness, strength and love. And we will be changed, little by little, into the image of Jesus.

Towards the end of this set of notes, we have the privilege of entering the wonderful Easter story once again. However you are approaching the start of this year, take a moment to remember the good news of Jesus Christ, proclaimed afresh each season: the message that Jesus has made a way back to the Father for every one of us; that our brokenness, shame and hurt is absorbed in his incredible act of sacrifice on the cross; and that his faithfulness and love towards you and me is the same, yesterday, today and forever. Welcome into a new year with Jesus!

BRF would like to hear from you! Complete our short survey for the chance to win a FREE subscription! Let us know what you like about BRF's Bible reading notes and how we can improve them to help more people encounter God through the Bible. Go to **brfonline.org.uk/BRNSURVEY**

Ezekiel: the glory of the Lord

Amy Boucher Pye writes:

Happy eighth day of Christmas, and happy New Year! For those of you seeking to embrace the twelve days of Christmas, I'm afraid that these notes on the book of Ezekiel will not feel terribly celebratory at times. This Old Testament prophet had a tough commission at a key point in the life of God's people, when God becomes so fed up that he takes them out of Jerusalem and removes his presence from the temple, his earthly home, while allowing its destruction. And Ezekiel, in conveying to the Israelites God's displeasure with them, suffers. Not only is he ostracised by his own people, but he endures, as a sign to the Israelites, being struck mute for five years and the horrible experience of his wife dying. But if you can hold on through the difficult readings, we will reach the hopeful ones at the end.

As a priest, Ezekiel should be serving in Jerusalem, but because of their sins the Israelites are exiled away from this special place where God made himself known. They fully expect to return there, never dreaming that God will remove himself from the temple. But he appears to them while in exile, which is surely a hopeful sign.

Another reason that this book can feel difficult relates to the apocalyptic visions that this prophet witnesses. But the book's structure will help us in understanding it, for it falls into three sections: first, chapters 1—24, in which Ezekiel prophesies against God's people; second, chapters 25—32, which are prophecies against other nations; and third, chapters 33—48, the prophecies of hope, salvation and blessing for the Israelites. We'll spend five days in the first section, one day in the second, and five days in the last.

Our readings illustrate that we, too, are like the Israelites – we can fall into sinful ways as we forget about or ignore God. But he redeems us and calls us back to himself, giving us help and hope through the indwelling of his Holy Spirit. We, like the Israelites, can hold on to the promises of communion with God.

In writing these notes, I've appreciated help from Bible commentaries, and especially the engaging one by Christopher J H Wright, *The Message of Ezekiel* (IVP, 2001).

WEDNESDAY 1 JANUARY EZEKIEL 1:1–6, 2:1–8

Life-changing times

'The people to whom I am sending you are obstinate and stubborn. Say to them, "This is what the Sovereign Lord says." And whether they listen or fail to listen – for they are a rebellious people – they will know that a prophet has been among them.' (NIV)

Do you remember the Y2K phenomenon? As I had lived away from the States for a couple of years, I watched the fear-mongering over the impending computer-systems doom on the other side of the Atlantic with a new objectivity. When we hit the first day of the year 2000, the feared apocalypse didn't come, rendering those prophecies kaput.

But some prophecies are true, especially those in the Bible. In our whistle-stop tour of Ezekiel, we'll see how God appears to him and gives him a message for God's errant people. The mind-blowing nature of God's appearance to him by the Kebar River not only catches his attention but changes him. Having been educated as a priest, and taken into exile, he is shaken up by becoming a prophet. He has to bear knowing the temple where he formerly served will be destroyed. Despite the cost, Ezekiel obeys God's instruction to eat the scroll (3:1–3) – to ingest God's words – and become a prophet. Then he, like God, laments over the Israelites' sin.

The vision in chapter 1 is laden with symbolism that would have been rich for the original readers. For instance, the windstorm came from the north, the source of Judah's enemies; also, the original hearers of the prophecy would have recognised the living creatures as God's cherubim. What's especially telling in this vision is that God is in motion, not constrained to his temple – and he's coming to call his people to account.

As we start 2020, why not take some time to consider how God has appeared to you in the past, and how you have changed because of it? How would you like God to reveal himself to you this year?

'Each of the four living creatures had six wings… Day and night they never stop saying: "'Holy, holy, holy is the Lord God Almighty,' who was, and is, and is to come'" (Revelation 4:8).

AMY BOUCHER PYE

THURSDAY 2 JANUARY   **EZEKIEL 3:16–27**

The watching post

'Son of man, I have made you a watchman for the people of Israel; so hear the word I speak and give them warning from me.' (NIV)

Ezekiel is already living in exile, with many other of the Israelites, when God calls him as a prophet. Because of the sins of the people, they have been banished from the promised land. Not only are they idolatrous, but they are also complacent about God's love and provision. They don't believe, as I've mentioned, that God will allow his house to be destroyed. But the Lord reaches the end of his patience and will let his home on earth be demolished.

When God calls Ezekiel not only to deliver his message, but to be his watchman, he increases the prophet's responsibility for the wayward people. For if Ezekiel fails to pass along God's message, *he* will be responsible for their sins. If, however, he tells them what God is saying, and they still refuse to obey God, then they hold responsibility for their own sins. Ezekiel acts as a model of obedience, for he hears and obeys the Lord.

If we've received the gift of God's saving love, we too are entrusted with God's message. We can figuratively look out over the fields, as a watchman would, warning about the incoming bandits or animals who would steal the crops. That is, we can (lovingly and appropriately) alert people about how a self-centred lifestyle will lead to emptiness and dissatisfaction, and how instead we all find true contentment in Christ.

Although we have been given the commission to share the good news of Jesus, I don't believe that God holds us solely responsible for the salvation of others. In this instance, the prophet had a special role in God's redemptive plan. How do you see your responsibility? And how can you share God's love today?

Lord, help me to hear you and, when I hear you, to heed you. Give me joy in following you, knowing that you have my best interests at heart.

AMY BOUCHER PYE

FRIDAY 3 JANUARY **EZEKIEL 4**

Acting out a sign

'Now, son of man, take a block of clay, put it in front of you and draw the city of Jerusalem on it. Then lay siege to it: erect siege works against it, build a ramp up to it… This will be a sign to the people of Israel.' (NIV)

As readers, we're inspired by books and films that share stories of a person's amazing change away from a life of crime, gangs or greed to a life with Jesus. Whereas that person used to live with secrets and lies, now they exude love and care as they seek to honour God.

As God relays his prophecies against Jerusalem, he turns Ezekiel into a sort of anti-hero – opposite to the subjects of those inspirational stories. God so wants his people to understand the errors of their ways that he goes to what may seem like extreme measures to get their attention. In this first prophecy against Israel, he instructs Ezekiel to act out his message. The prophet is to take some clay and make known that it represents Jerusalem under siege. Ezekiel will place a strong wall between himself and the city and then turn his face away from Jerusalem, showing God's people symbolically that God is cutting off contact with them.

The second sign involves more from Ezekiel, for he eats a meagre diet of a few grains for over a year as day by day he symbolically bears the sins of the people by lying on his side (whether for the whole day or part of the day, we're not sure). When the Lord cuts off the food supply from Jerusalem later, the Israelites will remember Ezekiel's act. And hopefully, they will repent.

These sign-acts can be hard to understand, especially their effect on Ezekiel. We can remember, however, how much God loved the Israelites and how distraught he was over their disregard for him. Rather than cut them off completely, he took to extreme measures. Of course, he did that again when he sent his Son to die for us.

Father God, how your heart must grieve when I ignore you. I know you won't turn your face from me, for Jesus is my advocate before you. Help me to love and serve you daily.

AMY BOUCHER PYE

SATURDAY 4 JANUARY   **EZEKIEL 8**

Secret sins

And he said to me, 'Son of man, do you see what they are doing – the utterly detestable things the Israelites are doing here, things that will drive me far from my sanctuary? But you will see things that are even more detestable.' (NIV)

As part of God's revelation to Ezekiel, the prophet is taken by the Spirit of God from exile to the temple, where he sees an increasingly number of horrible practices that denigrate the name of God. It's like Ezekiel watches a film shot by a secret camera that reveals the idolatrous worship that is breaking God's heart. And this is the reason God leaves his temple house – he cannot coexist with false idols. He can no longer countenance his people not being committed fully to him.

In showing the people's secret sins to Ezekiel, God affirms that nothing is hidden from him. Although they exclaim that the Lord does not see them (v. 12), Ezekiel learns otherwise.

Note how Ezekiel meticulously dates his visions – it's the most precise record that we have from a prophet. His documentation would have helped the Israelites to accept the validity of the prophecies after they came true. When God allowed the temple to be destroyed, the remaining Israelites joined Ezekiel and the others in exile.

Today, God's holiness can sometimes be brushed off as the concern of zealots. But we can see how much God mourns when his people worship other gods – whether statues of gold, as in times past, or the current gods of self-reliance, success, relationships, and paid or voluntary work. As in the days of Ezekiel, he sees into our secret hiding places, wanting to shine a light on our wrongdoing so that we can be clean before him. He doesn't want to punish us, but wants us to return to his open arms, where he greets us with love. May we receive his grace this day.

'Therefore, since we have these promises, dear friends, let us purify ourselves from everything that contaminates body and spirit, perfecting holiness out of reverence for God' (2 Corinthians 7:1).

AMY BOUCHER PYE

SUNDAY 5 JANUARY   **EZEKIEL 24:15–27**

God's delight

The word of the Lord came to me: 'Son of man, with one blow I am about to take away from you the delight of your eyes. Yet do not lament or weep or shed any tears. Groan quietly; do not mourn for the dead.' (NIV)

We've come to an excruciatingly difficult part of Ezekiel's story, for again God uses him as a sign to the Israelites. Their hearts continue to be hardened against God as they ignore Ezekiel's calls to repentance. In a final act, as Jerusalem is under siege and soon the temple will be destroyed, God 'with one blow' takes away the delight of Ezekiel – his wife.

Biblical commentators believe that Ezekiel was in his early 30s and his wife probably in her early 20s. They were clearly devoted to each other by God's reference to her being the 'delight of his eyes' (v. 16). Although she had married him expecting the life of a priest's wife, she stood by him during his strange antics as a prophet – the times of being struck mute (as he is in this story), of extreme fasts, of being ostracised by his fellows.

He knows that she will die, but he cannot say anything. Neither can he mourn in the culturally acceptable manner, which would have included wailing and other displays of emotion. Instead, he is to say nothing. This, finally, will get God's people's attention. Ezekiel will be a living prophecy.

How can we reconcile this very difficult story with a God of grace? To be honest, I'm not sure. Many biblical commentators conclude that God indeed caused her death, which we find hard to understand.

I believe that we need to read this account as an expression of God's deep sorrow over the way his people – the delight of his eyes – had left him. He conveyed his excruciating pain at their betrayal through Ezekiel and his wife, a sign that would truly get their attention. And it did.

In Jesus, the ultimate 'delight of his eyes', we see just how far God will go to save us.

'For you know that it was not with perishable things such as silver or gold that you were redeemed… but with the precious blood of Christ, a lamb without blemish or defect' (1 Peter 1:18–19).

AMY BOUCHER PYE

MONDAY 6 JANUARY   **EZEKIEL 30:1–19**

One Lord only

'They will be desolate among desolate lands, and their cities will lie among ruined cities. Then they will know that I am the Lord, when I set fire to Egypt and all her helpers are crushed.' (NIV)

As I mentioned in the introduction, the structure of the book of Ezekiel helps us to understand his work as a prophet. After the achingly hard news of his wife's death, we move not to the prophecies of hope for Israel, but the oracles against nations other than Israel. Just as the people of God have to wait for his words of hope, so we the readers of Ezekiel join them in waiting.

Throughout these chapters in the middle section of the book of Ezekiel, we hear again and again the refrain, 'Then they will know that I am the Lord' (see, for instance, verses 8 and 19 in this text). Just as God removes his presence from his people in the temple because he is not being honoured as the one and only Lord, so too he wants to be acknowledged as God among the nations. He is active in the world so that all will know that he is God.

Ezekiel's prophecy against Egypt condemns them for not following God, for instead putting their trust in earthly leaders. As a result, God says 'no longer will there be a prince in Egypt' (v. 13), for he is more powerful than those he has created. This prophecy also informs the Israelites that they cannot hope for help or rescue from the Egyptians. They too need to trust the true and living God.

As we live in uncertain times politically, we can read these words from many centuries ago and confirm that our hope lies in God. He is the supreme ruler; he is the one we should trust wholeheartedly. Although earthly leaders may fail us, the living Lord will not.

'Do not put your trust in princes, in human beings, who cannot save. When their spirit departs… their plans come to nothing. Blessed are those… whose hope is in the Lord their God' (Psalm 146:3–5).

AMY BOUCHER PYE

TUESDAY 7 JANUARY EZEKIEL 34:11–31

God, our shepherd

'Then they will know that I, the Lord their God, am with them and that they, the Israelites, are my people, declares the Sovereign Lord. You are my sheep, the sheep of my pasture, and I am your God, declares the Sovereign Lord.' (NIV)

On Epiphany, when we celebrate the wise men giving gifts to Jesus, we turn from Ezekiel's pronouncements of judgement to God's promises of hope. And what beautiful promises they are – about God's people being the sheep and God himself the shepherd. They are repeated by Jesus when he said, 'I am the good shepherd; I know my sheep and my sheep know me – just as the Father knows me and I know the Father – and I lay down my life for the sheep' (John 10:14–15).

Although God's people have been led astray by earthly shepherds, the Lord reasserts his ownership over the flock – he himself 'will tend [his] sheep and have them lie down' (v. 15). He will lead them to a safe pasture, where they will find security and rest. No longer will they be plundered (v. 28); no longer will the savage beasts destroy them (v. 25).

Why does the Lord do this? Again, the refrain from the previous chapters: 'Then they will know that I, the Lord their God, am with them and that they… are my people' (v. 30). God wants his people to recognise that he is their creator and maker; he is their Lord; he is their good shepherd; he is their everything.

We can embrace the idyllic picture of sheep grazing in verdant pastures when we think of God as the good shepherd. He knows that, just like sheep, we can be a bit slow or stubborn, and that we need caring for and protecting. He wants to lead us to good pasture as he encircles us with boundary lines that have fallen in pleasant places (see Psalm 16:6).

Lord, you are the good shepherd who cares for me and meets my needs. Help me to follow you today, moment by moment.

AMY BOUCHER PYE

WEDNESDAY 8 JANUARY **EZEKIEL 36:18–36**

For God's sake

'This is what the Sovereign Lord says: It is not for your sake, people of Israel, that I am going to do these things, but for the sake of my holy name, which you have profaned among the nations where you have gone.' (NIV)

I'm guessing that many of us, when we think of the book of Ezekiel, might think of this wonderful passage from chapter 36, about God sprinkling clean water on his people as he cleanses all impurities (v. 25) and how he removes a heart of stone and replaces it with a heart of flesh (v. 26). I remember a friend praying these verses over me many years ago, and how the promise of a new heart spoke to me strongly about my identity in Christ.

Although God works through his word so wonderfully, bringing it alive to us so many years after it was written, let's not miss out on the context of this particular passage. Before God speaks about cleansing his people and restoring them, he says *why* he will do this – not for their sake, but for the sake of his holy name (v. 22). His name has been profaned among the nations, and he must reveal his holiness so that he can be respected and honoured. Although he will bring them back from famine, making the corn plentiful, he does it not for their sake (v. 32), but so that the nations will know that he is the Lord and that he is the one who restored them (v. 36).

When we are tempted to claim credit for our latest project, good relationship or other blessing, we can remember that God is the Lord, and we are fruitful and faithful because of his Spirit living within us. When we want to beat ourselves up for a failure, we can look to God – Father, Son and Spirit – and ask him for help and forgiveness. We honour and serve the living God.

Lord Jesus Christ, renew me and restore me, and make my heart tender and pliable. Wash me clean with your living water.

AMY BOUCHER PYE

THURSDAY 9 JANUARY   **EZEKIEL 37:1–14**

New life

'Prophesy to these bones and say to them, "Dry bones, hear the word of the Lord!… I will make breath enter you, and you will come to life. I will attach tendons to you and make flesh come upon you… Then you will know that I am the Lord."' (NIV)

Do you remember a few days ago, when we read that the Spirit of God lifted Ezekiel and showed him the idolatry in the temple? He saw detestable things, sights that made him lament. I wonder what he thought when again the Spirit of the Lord transports him to the middle of a great valley. One commentator imagines a war scene, of bodies discarded here and there, left to rot. Ezekiel sees bones that are very dry, with no life left in them.

The God of the impossible asks Ezekiel if they can live, to which he replies wisely, 'Sovereign Lord, you alone know' (v. 3). Ezekiel has learnt that God alone creates life, and can even spark life where there is death. Ezekiel might have to stretch his belief to think that those bones can yet live, but he trusts that the Lord will bring them back to life.

Note how God involves Ezekiel in the resurrection – he is the one to prophesy to them, telling them to hear the word of the Lord and come back to life (v. 4). He calls on the four winds to come as the breath of life (v. 9). He prophesies that God will open the graves of the dead and bring them back to the land of Israel (v. 12).

The Lord who removed his presence from the temple yet restores his people. He doesn't want them to languish or rot, but wants them to live.

Consider your own life, and any areas that might feel dead and lifeless. Could you ask God to spark life in them – even though you may feel that's impossible?

'Forget the former things; do not dwell on the past. See, I am doing a new thing! Now it springs up; do you not perceive it? I am making a way in the wilderness and streams in the wasteland' (Isaiah 43:18–19).

AMY BOUCHER PYE

FRIDAY 10 JANUARY   **EZEKIEL 43:1–12**

Face down

Then the man brought me to the gate facing east, and I saw the glory of the God of Israel coming from the east. His voice was like the roar of rushing waters… The glory of the Lord entered the temple through the gate facing east. (NIV)

Once again, Ezekiel experiences a mystical trip in the Spirit, this time seeing the temple being rebuilt. When he understands that the dimensions are perfect, he senses that the time is coming soon for God to dwell with his people again, and that he will send his Spirit to live in the temple once more. And this is what Ezekiel is shown. God's glory comes from the east, and although years have passed since Ezekiel's first vision by the River Kebar, he falls face down in awe and wonder at the glory of God (v. 3). His many direct experiences of God can't take away from the mind-blowing nature of a new revelation.

After the Spirit picks him back up, he witnesses the glory of the Lord filling the temple and hears the promises that God will no longer leave them. Ezekiel will bear witness to all that he sees – not only the glory of God, but the perfection of the temple and the instructions to the Israelites on how to honour and glorify the Lord.

At God's holiness, Ezekiel falls in worship. His experience reminds us, too, that God is utterly holy. We might sometimes take him for granted, or assume he'll automatically forgive us when we do wrong. But when we ask him to increase our understanding of him, along with a holy fear of him, we renew a right sense of wonder and awe that the creator of the universe would seek our praise.

How today could you spend some time honouring God and worshiping his majesty? For some, visiting a grand church or cathedral might help them lift their eyes and hearts in awe. Others might experience the same sense of wonder in creation. May we join our hearts and minds in praise to God.

Lord, you promised not to remove your Spirit from your people, a promise you fulfilled with the coming of the Holy Spirit at Pentecost. Live in me this day.

AMY BOUCHER PYE

SATURDAY 11 JANUARY   **EZEKIEL 47:1–12**

The river of life

This water flows towards the eastern region and goes down into the Arabah, where it enters the Dead Sea. When it empties into the sea, the salty water there becomes fresh. Swarms of living creatures will live wherever the river flows. (NIV)

One of my favourite walks in north London is by a babbling brook. Some days the water looks murky and brown, but often it's crystal clear, flowing with freshness and energy. When I focus on the sounds of the moving water, I can forget that I'm close to a major metropolis. I can think about God's promises of living water and the river of life.

We close with Ezekiel's wonderful vision of a life-giving water, which flows symbolically out of the temple. The source of this water is God, who sends this river to cleanse the land that has been pillaged and abused, washing away the sins of God's people while bringing new life and hope. 'Swarms of living creatures will live wherever the river flows' (v. 9). God delights to turn water that is not suitable for drinking into something clean and refreshing: to take the old and make it new.

God promises his people living water in the New Testament as well. Jesus, during a great feast, said that those who believed in him would have 'rivers of living water' flow from within them (John 7:38), by which he meant the Holy Spirit. Those who follow him have received this life-giving gift.

As you think back to the opening days of 2020 and our journey with Ezekiel, consider what struck you most about this prophet. Did God speak to you through him? Perhaps today you can act on some of the insights or lessons that you've learned.

I hope you will join me in praising God for sending Jesus, the living water, to cleanse us and quench our thirst. May we share this wonderful source of life with those whom we meet, and may we remain awed at the glory and wonder of God.

'On each side of the river stood the tree of life, bearing twelve crops of fruit, yielding its fruit every month. And the leaves of the tree are for the healing of the nations' (Revelation 22:2).

AMY BOUCHER PYE

A letter to the Romans

Christine Platt writes:

Romans is an expansive, wide-ranging letter. Neither Paul nor any of the apostles had personally visited the church in Rome. Paul planned to go there, so to prepare for his visit he decided to give the Christians in Rome a thorough explanation of the gospel of Jesus – something they could chew on prior to his arrival.

The church in Rome was most probably started by people who'd believed in Jesus at Pentecost. It was composed of both Jews and Gentiles. One of the main themes Paul covers is how both Jews and Gentles have a place together in God's plan for humanity.

The first eleven chapters cover the facts – what we need to believe. Paul had spent many years under God's tutelage to refine his theological understanding and we get the benefit of that. However, we know that Paul was never content with just theory, and the same applies to God! Belief in God through theory alone is meaningless. As with everything in life, knowledge and understanding are vital foundation stones; but they are of little use if there is no practical outworking, except to make us feel proud of our knowledge. The final five chapters of Romans cover how we should behave, having understood and been convinced of the facts.

The first major theme is sin, of which we have daily evidence in our own lives, others' lives and on the world's stage. Dwelling on sin can get 'heavy', but it's important not to minimise our sinful state. We need to allow that 'heaviness' to impact us, so we appreciate more deeply our need of a Saviour.

If at any time during the readings you feel overwhelmed or overburdened by your or someone else's sin, keep also in mind the key verse, Romans 5:1: 'Therefore, since we have been made right in God's sight by faith, we have peace with God because of what Jesus Christ our Lord has done for us' (NLT). Whereas the human predicament is ghastly, the remedy is utterly glorious and freely available to all without any human effort being necessary.

Paul did eventually get to Rome. He visited twice – both times as a prisoner under Roman guard. Despite the hindrances imposed on him there, he had a deeply significant ministry and wrote several letters from there – Ephesians, Philippians, Colossians and Philemon, and possibly others.

SUNDAY 12 JANUARY ROMANS 1:7–25

Look around you

God shows his anger from heaven against all sinful, wicked people who suppress the truth… For ever since the world was created, people have seen the earth and sky. Through everything God made, they can clearly see his invisible qualities… So they have no excuse for not knowing God. (NLT)

Do you remember a time when natural beauty took your breath away? One crisp sunny afternoon when skiing on a mountain in Switzerland, I stopped and gasped in awe. I was completely alone; my friends were ahead of me. I crested a slope and all before me was glistening white untouched snow. Each crystal twinkled and there was deep silence. The sight touched me profoundly. It was otherworldly.

A few years later, when I finally gave my life to Jesus, I remembered that moment and thanked God for 'knocking on the door of my heart' even though it took me a while to open it.

God longs to communicate with us and he has placed this intricately designed and finely balanced world in this universe for us to live in. He has done everything to reveal himself: the natural world, sending the prophets and – the ultimate proof – Jesus. None of us has any excuse for remaining ignorant about God.

It is clear, however, that there are those who want to suppress the truth. They not only resist God for themselves but also want to rob others of the opportunity to know him. But God will not allow himself to be gagged. Day by day, he still provides spectacular glories in earth and sky, shouting to a somnolent world – 'Here I am!' His handiwork is evident for those with open eyes to see him.

How much more would we know about God if we took more time and attention to 'smell the roses'; to really examine the detail of tree bark, of a fuchsia, of a chaffinch; or to savour the sunset, asking God, 'What are you showing me through this?'

Take a walk, or look out of your window. What can you see of God's invisible qualities – something of his power, his attention to detail, his creativity, his love of beauty and colour? Enjoy it and be thankful.

CHRISTINE PLATT

MONDAY 13 JANUARY   **ROMANS 2**

God is kind, but not soft

Did you think that because he's such a nice God, he'd let you off the hook?… God is kind, but he's not soft. In kindness he takes us firmly by the hand and leads us into a radical life-change… Every refusal and avoidance of God adds fuel to the fire. (MSG)

On his deathbed in 1856, the German poet Heinrich Heine stated: 'God will forgive me. It's his job.' I wonder what he said when he met God face-to-face. It's comforting to have an image of God as a doting father who overlooks every time his child disobeys. Yet such children are generally obnoxious to be around and grow up to be selfish adults who think the world owes them a living. Nobody applauds parents who spoil their children, so why would we expect God to do that?

Every wise parent knows there must be consequences for misbehaviour. God is no exception. He lets us know what the results of a life of wilful sin will be. 'Make no mistake: In the end you get what's coming to you – *Real Life* for those who work on God's side, but to those who insist on getting their own way and take the path of least resistance, *Fire!*' (v. 7).

On the other hand, God is kind. He is not a celestial policeman with his baton raised ready to rap our knuckles when we fail. Forgiveness is freely available to those who repent. If Heinrich had said: 'God will forgive me when I repent and turn away from doing wrong,' he would have been a much wiser man.

God is immeasurably kind and he is also utterly fair and just. He has clearly warned humanity of the outcome of turning away from his loving presence. Those who resist his compassion and his plans will find themselves facing an unspeakably dire aftermath.

I'm sure we've all resisted parental instruction, partly because we didn't understand that it was meant for our good. God's instructions are always given to protect us and to benefit us.

Merciful God, help me not to abuse your kindness by treating sin lightly. Grant me sensitivity to your Holy Spirit so I will be quick to confess when I've done wrong and turn away from disobedience.

CHRISTINE PLATT

TUESDAY 14 JANUARY ROMANS 3:21–31, 4:1–8, 18–25

Earned or free?

For everyone has sinned; we all fall short of God's glorious standard. Yet God, in his grace, freely makes us right in his sight. He did this through Christ Jesus when he freed us from the penalty for our sins. (NLT)

Paul writes to Jews who were steeped in God's law and were convinced that obedience was the key to God's approval and acceptance. He also writes to Gentiles (like most of us) who similarly have a sense that we need to earn our way through life.

In the 1970s, when I was first a nurse, we cared for our patients and had regular reports done on us to check we were doing a good job. As years went by, increasingly we seemed to have to prove our worth to the health authorities – forms and more forms, assessments and more assessments!

Not so with God. There is no celestial form-filling, or filing cabinets, or iCloud crammed with progress reports on us. 'People are counted as righteous, not because of their work, but because of their faith in God who forgives sinners' (Romans 4:5).

Paul knows this is hard for humanity to grasp, so he uses the illustration of Abraham, who believed God and was declared righteous. Abraham was an exceptional example of faith, yet he also had some moral lapses. Humanly speaking, he wouldn't have had a perfect scorecard, but his faith, not his works, was the vital component.

Because we're programmed to earn acceptance, it can be difficult for us to accept God's love and forgiveness as a free gift. Many of us are sceptical of free gifts offered by advertisers. And Satan doesn't want us to enjoy the freedom of salvation by faith alone. He will constantly remind us of our shortcomings and goad us to feel guilty and try harder. Yet, if we continue to strive to win God's approval in our own strength, we nullify all that Jesus did for us.

God, my loving Father, and Jesus, my glorious redeemer and Saviour, I accept again today your free gift of being made holy in your sight. I am accepted. I am holy. I am loved. Thank you so much.

CHRISTINE PLATT

Peace and joy – where are they?

We can rejoice, too, when we run into problems and trials, for we know that they help us develop endurance. And endurance develops strength of character, and character strengthens our confident hope of salvation. (NLT)

In the NIV 1984 translation, this chapter is entitled 'Peace and joy' – both of which humanity craves. Many search for them in unhelpful and even destructive places. I remember hearing one expert claim that when drug addicts inject themselves, they are actually seeking heaven; instead, they find bondage, sickness and breakdown in relationships. They harm the people who love them and whom they love. Even those of us who look for peace and joy in our relationship with Jesus don't always experience this. So where are these delights to be found?

One would anticipate that if God's gift is peace and joy, he would naturally shield us from difficulties, hassles and pain. But we know, and daily experience shows us, that he does not do that. God's much-loved people hit many roadblocks, upsets and trauma.

Although we would love to be coddled and cosseted, with every need met and no hardships, God knows that would keep us immature and infantile. His desire is for us to develop endurance, strength of character and steadfast hope.

How does this miracle take place? By accepting and rejoicing in whatever problems come our way, trusting that God will work them out for our good and his pleasure.

I confess I find accepting a lot easier than rejoicing. Maybe this is why peace and joy are not my constant companions. I can accept that as I age, more limitations will be placed on my physical and mental abilities, but I find it hard to rejoice in that. This attitude can lead to fear – the opposite of peace and joy. The remedy is clear from scripture: let's focus on the positive outcome of our problems – endurance, character and hope, rather than the present pain and frustrations.

Think back to how God has developed you through past difficulties. Use this perspective to help you accept and rejoice in your current life situation.

CHRISTINE PLATT

THURSDAY 16 JANUARY   **ROMANS 6**

Living in freedom

Do not let sin control the way you live; do not give in to sinful desires… Instead, give yourselves completely to God, for you were dead, but now you have new life… Sin is no longer your master… Instead, you live under the freedom of God's grace. (NLT)

In this chapter, Paul calls for believers to become in experience what we already are in position. We are dead to sin; we are alive to God. 'Our old sinful selves were crucified with Christ so that sin might lose its power in our lives' (v. 6).

A vital step towards victory over sin is a decision to 'not give in to sinful desires'. We will experience temptation until the day we see Jesus face-to-face. There will be an ongoing battle to not give in. But we don't belong to that world any longer. We have emigrated to a new realm where Jesus' values and lifestyle reign supreme.

When I lived in Switzerland, I had to speak French. I couldn't cling on to my old familiar way of communicating. I had to embrace a new language and culture. Not that my English language and culture were sinful! How much more, therefore, should we discard our old sinful deeds and actively learn and train ourselves in God's values and ways?

Part of 'not giving in' involves surrendering to God, his purposes and his will. 'Throw yourselves wholeheartedly and full-time – remember you've been raised from the dead! – into God's way of doing things' (v. 13, MSG). Just as I had to listen carefully to my French teacher and do my homework, so we need to be attentive to our new teacher, the Holy Spirit, as he shows us daily how to live 'under the freedom of God's grace' (v. 14).

This total lifestyle change is infinitely more significant than learning a new language. Speaking French enabled me to live comfortably in Switzerland. Walking God's way prepares us for heaven and equips us to serve Jesus here on earth!

Sing or say this song to Jesus: 'All to Jesus I surrender, all to Him I freely give. I will ever love and trust him, in his presence daily live' (Judson W. Van DeVenter, 1855–1939).

CHRISTINE PLATT

FRIDAY 17 JANUARY　　　　　　　　　　　　　　　　　　**ROMANS 7**

Be prepared for war

You died to the power of the law when you died with Christ. And now you are united with the one who was raised from the dead. As a result, we can produce a harvest of good deeds for God. (NLT)

These verses make the Christian walk sound quite easy. We died with Christ, we are united with him in his resurrection, and a harvest of good deeds for God will follow – easy-peasy!

As we know the human experience is not so straightforward. We still have daily choices of whether to go God's way or not and Satan makes the alternative look quite appealing. It feels easier to tell that lie, or gossip, or give in to greed. They're just little sins, we say, and try to convince ourselves they don't matter in the long run. No one will know. But one lie can lead to many others and we quickly find ourselves caught in a tangled web of deception. Untamed greed wreaks havoc with our credit card or our waistline and health. It is far easier to stop something before it mushrooms into catastrophe for us and those around us.

Even with all that Jesus has done for us in dying for our sins and in breaking the power of Satan over our lives, we still find ourselves slipping into sinful patterns. It seems to come so naturally. But Jesus is ever the rescuer. However far we fall, we can always turn back, repent and start again on the right track, although we need to be careful not to abuse his kindness and love. It's vital to put some safeguards in place to prevent future disasters. Maybe some social situations or some entertainment channels are unhelpful. We could ask a good friend to hold us accountable. Whatever it takes, it is worth it to progress in God's kingdom ways and reap a harvest of good deeds for him. The alternative is a wasted life, and much sorrow for us and our friends and families.

Think about areas of temptation for you. What sets you off down the wrong road? How can you avoid these in future and be better prepared to face the war against sin? Ask a friend or a pastor for help.

CHRISTINE PLATT

SATURDAY 18 JANUARY   **ROMANS 8:1–4, 12–39**

Chosen, called, made holy, glorified

And having chosen them, he called them to come to him. And having called them, he gave them right standing with himself. And having given them right standing, he gave them his glory. (NLT)

Every generation of loving parents wants to give their children more opportunities to progress in life than they themselves received. My father was keen for my sisters and me to learn to play the piano. He missed out on music lessons as a child and he strove to give us the best. Sadly, he miscalculated and didn't take into consideration my lack of musical ability! However, my more gifted sisters benefitted greatly.

God as our heavenly parent also has high goals for his children. He chose us. The Amplified Bible translation of Ephesians 1:4 expresses it this way: '[in His love] He chose us in Christ [actually selected us for Himself as His own]'. None of us is just an anonymous face in the crowd. We are especially chosen for himself. What expansive, extravagant love!

We are called – not to failure or mediocrity – but to come to God; to be ushered with honour into the throne room; to be greeted with joy and delight. And in that place, we receive right standing with God: 'I am overwhelmed with joy in the Lord my God! For he has dressed me with the clothing of salvation and draped me in a robe of righteousness' (Isaiah 61:10) – completely covered and made holy.

Glory – this brings to mind Jesus' transfiguration. In Matthew, we read: 'Jesus' appearance was transformed so that his face shone like the sun, and his clothes became as white as light' (17:2). It was as though the curtains of heaven parted and revealed a precious glimpse of the glory we will share when Jesus returns. This final stage of the process is set in God's purposes and therefore it is stated as though it has already happened – 'he gave them his glory'.

Father God, thank you that I have been chosen, I have been called to come to you, I have been made holy and I will be glorified. Help me to remember these amazing truths in my daily life.

CHRISTINE PLATT

SUNDAY 19 JANUARY ROMANS 9:22–33, 10:1–15

Beautiful feet

Jew and Gentile are the same in this respect. They have the same Lord, who gives generously to all who call on him… How can they believe in him if they have never heard about him? And how can they hear about him unless someone tells them? (NLT)

Paul desperately wanted his people, the Jewish race, to receive Christ as their long-awaited Messiah and redeemer. The Jewish people had the privilege of being God's first choice. They received the prophets and the scriptures. God appeared to them while they wandered the wilderness, and Jesus was Jewish in his human ancestry. Despite all this, many still refused to accept that Jesus was the one for whom they had been waiting, and tragically even to this day many are still waiting.

Those of us who are Gentiles have much to thank the Jewish people for, especially in their careful guardianship and study of the scriptures. I've had the opportunity to attend a Passover feast, led by a Jewish believer in Christ who explained the significance of all its aspects. That was enriching and enlightening.

Even though the Jews were called first, Gentiles are now also included in God's magnificent plan of salvation. 'Everyone who calls on the name of the Lord will be saved' (10:13). But neither Jews nor Gentiles can respond to God's merciful invitation until they hear about it, which is where our beautiful feet come in (Isaiah 52:7). Whatever the state of your physical feet (mine are not my most attractive feature), they actually become spiritually beautiful when you walk across the road or travel to another country to share the salvation message of Jesus.

The longing of Paul's heart and his prayer to God was for the Jewish people to be saved. Who is on your heart? For whom do you pray that they might hear and understand the gospel? This is where prayer and action fit together. We pray and we walk on our beautiful feet to tell others about Jesus and show his reality by the way we live.

Compassionate God, I bring _____ to you. Please give me opportunities to share something of you with them this week. Give me courage and the right words to say and help me love them as you do.

CHRISTINE PLATT

MONDAY 20 JANUARY ROMANS 11:11–36

God's mighty mysterious mind

Oh, how great are God's riches and wisdom and knowledge! How impossible it is for us to understand his decisions and his ways! For who can know the Lord's thoughts? Who knows enough to give him advice? (NLT)

Do you ever feel confused when you read the Bible? Some aspects of theology are hard to grasp. Paul's explanation about the position of Jews and Gentiles is complex. The main gist is that, despite coming from totally different backgrounds, both Jews and Gentiles now have access to God's mercy and forgiveness and can enter into his kingdom. We are not told when or how that will happen, or who will accept his love, or who will continue to reject him. These remain deep mysteries.

Having done his best to explain, Paul's response to complex issues is to burst out in praise to God as he realises afresh how awesome is God's grace. His gigantic plan of salvation encompasses everyone who has ever lived or who will ever live. When you are unsure or have questions about God's ways, it's always constructive to get back to basics and remind yourself that God knows what he is doing and his plan is perfect. His mind is on a vastly different dimension to ours, so how could we possibly understand his decisions, his ways or his thoughts (Isaiah 55:8–9)? Thinking of God's perfection should lead us to praise rather than leave us in a state of confusion.

This does not mean that we put our brains to sleep and don't ask questions or seek understanding, but we need to keep the reality of God's constant love and wisdom in the forefront of our minds. 'Who knows enough to give him advice?' He can actually run the universe without our assistance! It is because of his mercy that he invites us to participate in his kingdom-building by prayer and service.

Meditate on Isaiah 55:8–9: '"My thoughts are nothing like your thoughts," says the Lord. "And my ways are far beyond anything you could imagine."' Take comfort in God's complete understanding of your questions and burdens.

CHRISTINE PLATT

TUESDAY 21 JANUARY   ROMANS 12

Working well together

We are many parts of one body, and we all belong to each other. In his grace, God has given us different gifts for doing certain things well. (NLT)

Four years ago I fractured my wrist. I was in plaster for about seven weeks. That injury really hampered the good functioning of my body. Getting dressed with one hand is an exercise in purposeful wriggling! But, with the passage of time and a skilful physio, it came right and my body was relieved and appreciated the renewed agility. Paul likens Christians to the body of Christ (v. 4–5). When all the parts work well together, it's magnificent, but a part that is out of action spoils the whole.

God's plan for the people who form Christ's body on earth is to give each of us 'different gifts for doing certain things well'. You may be like me in wishing you'd received different gifts. I'd love to be better at hospitality and music, but no. I can try my best, but they are certainly not areas I excel in.

But I do like writing, admin and teaching. I need to be happy with what God has given and develop those gifts as much as possible, rather than waste time and energy trying to do or be something or someone I'm not. Developing our gifts takes effort. 'Never be lazy, but work hard and serve the Lord enthusiastically' (v. 11).

Gifts are precious, but without the fundamental attitude of offering ourselves to God as a 'living and holy sacrifice' (v. 1), they can make us proud or dismissive of our God-given strengths. We either start to think how impressive we are – 'Gosh, I did that well' – or consider ourselves worthless – 'I can't do anything. I'm no use to anyone.' Both extremes deny the generosity and wisdom of God. He knows how best we can contribute to his kingdom on earth.

Have you identified your gifts? You may need to ask a friend to help you. What steps are you taking to develop them? Present them and yourself to God for his use and pleasure.

CHRISTINE PLATT

WEDNESDAY 22 JANUARY   **ROMANS 13**

Honour your government!

Everyone must submit to governing authorities. For all authority comes from God, and those in positions of authority have been placed there by God… Pay your taxes and government fees to those who collect them, and give respect and honour to those who are in authority. (NLT)

In the last election in New Zealand, the result was not the one I voted for. I was upset and angry. As time went on, I found myself waiting gleefully for any mistakes the new government was making. Not a helpful attitude!

Even though there are several different interpretations of verses 1–7, they did challenge my feelings and beliefs. I knew I needed to pray for the government and that was a struggle, but it's taken me a while to trust that our present leaders are the ones God has permitted to rule us at this time.

When Paul was writing about 2,000 years ago, the government he referred to was secular and certainly had its flaws, but Paul says, despite that, we should respect and honour those in authority.

'The authorities are God's servants, sent for your good' (v. 4). Their role is to maintain good order. I think many politicians would be shocked to find themselves classed as God's servants! However, if these authorities fail in their responsibilities, or compel citizens to disobey God's laws, we must respectfully resist as Peter did in Acts 5:29: 'We must obey God rather than any human authority.' God-fearing men and women throughout the centuries have opposed corrupt governments and suffered horrendously. We need courageous discernment to know how and when to resist.

The encouragement Paul gives in verses 11–14 is that this world system has a limited time span. One day, maybe soon, Jesus will return and establish his model government. While we wait, we need to be dependable and loyal citizens and work for the prosperity and well-being of the country God has placed us in, praying that our leaders will acknowledge God as head of all authority.

Do you, like me, need to renew your commitment to pray regularly for your government leaders? Instead of fretting or complaining, we can bring our concerns to God and ask for his help in how to influence decisions.

CHRISTINE PLATT

THURSDAY 23 JANUARY   **ROMANS 14**

Tend to your own knitting!

Yes, each of us will give a personal account to God. So let's stop condemning each other. Decide instead to live in such a way that you will not cause another believer to stumble and fall. (NLT)

I'm sure you'll agree that if we could eliminate wanton criticism from the world, it would be a much happier and peaceful place. I'm convinced it would also contribute vastly to everyone's emotional and mental well-being. If changing the whole world seems out of reach, we should at least be aiming towards a criticism-free Christian world.

Believers in Paul's time were disagreeing over what food they should eat and whether certain days were more holy than others. Today, we may argue about other issues – style of worship music, what to do on Sundays, alcohol consumption, tattoos, etc. Human beings seem to be highly inventive in finding ways to criticise and judge each other and it's sad and disappointing when it occurs in the Christian community.

How to combat this? In *The Message* translation, Romans 14:12 reads: 'So tend to your knitting. You've got your hands full just taking care of your own life before God.' We are accountable to God for our own conduct, not that of other people. God doesn't give us the right or responsibility to find fault with our fellow believers. We need to concentrate on sorting out our own lives before God – then we won't have time or energy to condemn or judge others.

We should focus instead on living exemplary lives so that we don't offend our Christian brothers and sisters or lead them astray by our behaviour. This requires us to be sensitive to others' needs and beliefs. After all, one day all of us will together bow the knee before Jesus and these differences of opinion will fade into oblivion. We will be ashamed and wonder why we ever argued over such trivial matters.

Father God forgive me for being critical of _____. Help me to accept, understand and try to see things from their point of view. Please strengthen and guide me to set a good example for others to follow.

CHRISTINE PLATT

FRIDAY 24 JANUARY   **ROMANS 15:1–29**

Christ – servant to the Jews

Remember that Christ came as a servant to the Jews to show that God is true to the promises he made to their ancestors. He also came so that the Gentiles might give glory to God for his mercies to them. (NLT)

I find it fascinating that you can read scripture time and time again and suddenly get a fresh insight from verses that are already very familiar. This happened for me with the above text.

Maybe those of us who are Gentiles are so used to enjoying the fact that Jesus came to die for the sins of the whole world that we forget that his earthly ministry focused mainly on Jewish people. He came 'as a servant to the Jews' and to be the fulfilment of promises made to their ancestors, not to Gentile ancestors. I'd never really grasped that before. It is wonderfully true that Jesus always kept all of humanity in view, but his first focus was the Jews. God the Father's plan of salvation always had the Jews in the forefront.

Paul emphasises this in verses 25–27. The Gentile believers in Macedonia and Achaia heard that the believers in Jerusalem were in dire straits financially. They gathered together a monetary gift and asked Paul to deliver it for them. Paul explains that this was in fact their responsibility. They had received spiritual blessings from the Jerusalem community and so, in turn, needed to care for their material needs. 'Since the Gentiles received the spiritual blessings of the Good News from the believers in Jerusalem, they feel the least they can do in return is to help them financially.'

On the other hand, Galatians 3:28–29 contains this staggering promise: 'There is no longer Jew or Gentile, slave or free, male and female. For you are all one in Christ Jesus… You are his heirs, and God's promise to Abraham belongs to you.' Keeping both these truths in mind, I still wonder whether the Gentile Christian world needs to develop a deeper concern for Jewish people.

You may not know any Jewish people personally, but could you consider including the Jewish people around the world in your prayers?

CHRISTINE PLATT

SATURDAY 25 JANUARY   **ROMANS 16**

Clean the toilet with joy!

Give my greetings to Mary, who has worked so hard… I, Tertius, the one writing this letter for Paul, send my greetings, too… Gaius says hello to you. He is my host and also serves as host to the whole church. (NLT)

This chapter paints a picture of everyone working together, carrying out the roles for which God had gifted and called them. Gaius was a generous host from whom the whole church benefitted. No doubt his family and servants did the cooking and cleaning! This enabled Paul's ministry to prosper and Gaius to play his part. Tertius acted as Paul's secretary. This is the only mention of him in the New Testament.

In my early working life, I was a secretary. Even though in those days we were poorly paid and often overlooked, without our help our bosses would have floundered. Mary worked hard, as did many others.

Without this back-up crew, Paul and the whole early church would have been severely limited, and we may never have been able to read this letter. God had called Paul to a specific ministry and he also gave him an impressive support staff. When God calls, he provides. Some roles were upfront, others were backstage, but all were vital. Paul is eager to express his appreciation of their efforts and contribution.

In reality, the person who cleans the church toilets is just as necessary as the worship leader or the preacher. I wonder how often the cleaner or the admin staff get thanked.

Living in a hierarchical world where our value is often assessed by the role we play, it's easy to overlook the helpers doing the seemingly humdrum work, but Paul didn't overlook them and neither does Jesus. We aren't all gifted in the same way, but we all have our essential part to play and we are equally valued by Jesus. So, we can hold our heads high as we do the supremely important job of cleaning the toilets!

Thank God for the opportunities you have to serve, even if no one else notices. Be assured that God is delighted and appreciates your contribution. Try to find ways of thanking others who serve you.

CHRISTINE PLATT

Rest

Jean Watson writes:

> What is rest?
>   Is it pausing to savour sensory delights:
>   awesome creativity in art and nature?
> Is it human interconnectedness
>   harmonious converse, healing laughter?
> Is it ringing the changes
>   from doing to being – from active to still,
>   to playful, creative awareness?
> Is it finding soul space
>   for realising, relishing
>   our countless causes for gratitude:
>   for life, for being alive here and now;
> for extravagant love offered, received,
>   creating life's meaning;
> for seeing, with faith's eyes,
>   how your creative, relational
>   model of working and resting,
>   is even now moving
>   this sometimes grim, sometimes glorious
>   cosmic creation adventure
>   towards its planned,
>   its perfect close?

SUNDAY 26 JANUARY   **GENESIS 2:2–3**

God rests

By the seventh day God had finished the work he had been doing, so on the seventh day he rested from all his work. (NIV)

We think today about God resting after his active work of creation and what that might suggest for our own lives. In our quoted verse, using inadequate human language to aid our understanding, the writer tells us that God rested after work. And we know it was creative work: 'In the beginning God created' (Genesis 1:1).

What could 'rest' following God's example mean for us?

- It might give us the chance to reflect on what we have done, our work, and say, 'This is good.' (If it is!)
- It might also give us a chance to do something different, to have a change of pace, scene, focus or activity in our lives.
- Crucially, it gives us the space to worship and relate to God in the company of his people.

Throughout the Bible, God is depicted as very active. He acts in the cosmos, in nature, in the lives of nations and individuals. So it's good to have this reminder of God resting. But what about this verse: 'He who watches over Israel will neither slumber nor sleep' (Psalm 121:3)? This is metaphorical language and certainly doesn't mean that God never rests. Interpreting this in the context of the whole Bible, I believe the message is that God doesn't switch off, stop being himself when he is resting; he still sees, watches over, takes ultimate responsibility for all he has made and cares for.

How about your own way of resting? Could it be that you need to adjust to *doing* less and *being* more? Or perhaps God is calling you to a different and – for you as an individual – more enjoyable and creative kind of *doing*?

In the rhythm of your life, is there creative/recreative rest? If not, could you plan for it in your daily schedule, starting today?

JEAN WATSON

MONDAY 27 JANUARY   **MARK 6:30–34**

Time out with Jesus

'**Come with me by yourselves to a quiet place and get some rest.**' (NIV)

In yesterday's passage, there was a picture of God resting after creative work. Today, Jesus, God in human form, invites his close friends to take time out with him. What an invitation! Let's break it down:

'*Come with me*': What a difference it makes when someone says, 'Come with me' rather than, 'You go' or 'You should go'.

'*By yourselves*': Away from other people and, away from other situations and activities.

'*To a quiet place*': Away from noise and bustle and busyness. Perhaps to a place where the beauty and variety of creation can delight and lift our spirits.

'*And get some rest*': Some suggested synonyms for rest are: take time out, slow down, relax, ease up, pause, have a break, unwind, take it easy, luxuriate.

For the disciples, it was Jesus who issued this invitation. Do you think it was just for them or that, through this story, he is inviting all his followers and friends to take time out with him?

What had the disciples been doing? They had been accompanying Jesus as he went about doing good: preaching, teaching, having one-to-ones with individuals, feeding five thousand people; in other words, doing a lot of walking, meeting people's needs, being busy and active. They must have been longing for rest so that they could slow down, be still, have a break, unwind and – since they were with Jesus – luxuriate: be blessed and reinspired.

How do you, could you, take time out with Jesus? Many people have found that joining a small group for a sensitively led quiet morning can be a good way of doing this. But we can take time out with Jesus on our own – perhaps a little time each day, or a longer time now and again, or both.

A suggestion: Tell Jesus which aspects of rest you most need and why at this time in your life – and then listen, listen, listen…

JEAN WATSON

TUESDAY 28 JANUARY EXODUS 20:8–10

Just one holy, restful day?

Remember the Sabbath day by keeping it holy… On it you shall not do any work. (NIV)

The people of God had specific instructions about the sabbath – Saturday. It was to be holy and free from work. Over time, the number of things that the people of God were *not* to do on that day came to outnumber the things they *were* to do.

But by the first century in the early church, the day for worship changed from the seventh to the first day of the week. The believers met for worship on the 'Lord's day' – Sunday, the day on which Jesus had risen from the dead (see Acts 20:7).

So as the day changed, the emphasis changed too. Sunday was not about what the believers mustn't do but about what they did do. They gathered together for worship. Jesus had already taught that sabbath-keeping should never been about ticking do and don't boxes, but about honouring God and doing good (Luke 13:10–17). Similarly, Sunday was to be a holy day, a day set apart for worship, fellowship and compassion: the 'Lord's day' in which a change of pace, focus and activity would provide rest and refreshment for mind, body and spirit.

However, is it enough, or even biblical, to treat just one day in seven as the Lord's day and the rest of the week as my day, my time? Would our perspectives and priorities change if we were to treat every day as the Lord's day – a day in which, whether we are working or resting, Jesus and his priorities are central?

Some people have to work on Sundays, so cannot make that particular day, or even any other day, a day solely for rest. But they – and we – could, instead, make rest part of the rhythm of each 'holy' day (i.e. every day) – as I think our psalm tomorrow suggests.

For thought and prayer: Where are you on the spectrum of a holy, restful Sunday and a secular/busy week, or a Sunday which inspires and refreshes you for how you want to live the rest of the week?

JEAN WATSON

WEDNESDAY 29 JANUARY   **PSALM 23**

Rest as part of the rhythm of life

He makes me lie down in green pastures, he leads me beside quiet waters, he refreshes my soul. (NIV)

I rather like *The Message* translation here: 'You have bedded me down in lush meadows, you find me quiet pools to drink from. True to your word, you let me catch my breath and send me in the right direction.'

In this psalm, we have a picture of a shepherd and of a king – the rod and the staff or crook were symbols of kingship. Both apply to David, who in his youth shepherded his father's flock and, later, as Israel's king shepherded the people of God. Yet in this psalm the writer, probably David, is addressing God as the shepherd-king who is taking care of him, the sheep. This picture of God as shepherd to an individual sheep is striking; more frequently in the Old Testament God is seen as the shepherd of his people.

Christians down the ages have derived enormous help and comfort from this psalm, not just as the people of God together but as individual Christians. What can you count on, as an individual, according to this psalm? Read it again. To me, it speaks of God's care, protection and provision – including nourishment and refreshment – amid all the changing scenes of each of our lives, especially when we meet the dark valleys of want, hardship, injury and even death.

Do you really believe this for yourself as 'the sheep'?

Fresh grass and still waters – or lush meadows and quiet pools – are part of the rhythm of the sheep's journey in this psalm. Quite literally these and other aspects of the natural world, created by God, can be a rich source of rest and renewal to us – as can play and creativity in any of their many forms.

For thought or prayer and perhaps action: What sort of scenes, situations, activities, relationships really rest, nourish and refresh – you?

JEAN WATSON

THURSDAY 30 JANUARY   **PSALM 37:1–7**

Developing a restful spirit

Be still before the Lord and wait patiently for him. (NIV)

Have you noticed that unless you have a restful spirit, you aren't able to get the full benefit of restful surroundings? This psalm, I think, suggests ways in which we can help to develop that restful spirit.

There are some clear dos and don'ts in our passage.

- Verses 1–2: Don't fret. Don't envy.

What do you find yourself fretting or being envious about? You may identify with what is mentioned in these verses, as Gerard Manley Hopkins did when he wrote, 'Why do sinners' ways prosper? And why must/Disappointment all I endeavour end?'

There is no answer in this life to the poet's question. The matters raised in these two verses are beyond our control. They are God's responsibility and he will deal with them in his time and way. Reminding ourselves of this could help us not to fret or be envious in relation to life's injustices and inequalities.

The other verses give us positives to reflect on.

- Verses 3–4: Trust and delight in God and do good.
- Verses 5–6: Commit your way to God. Trust in him.
- Verse 7: Be still before God. Wait patiently for him.

Reflect again on this list: Trust in God. Delight in God. Do good. Commit your way to God. Be still before God. Wait patiently for God. These are ways in which we can be helped not to fret or be envious; ways which can help to 'take from our lives the strain and stress', as one hymn puts it. I am sure that these dos and don'ts are *not* intended to make us feel guilty but rather to bless us: to bring us greater joy, peace and fullness of life as we learn to put them into practice.

What particularly strikes home to you in these verses? Focus on that in your praying and in identifying a way forward for you.

JEAN WATSON

FRIDAY 31 JANUARY
MATTHEW 11:28–30

Soul rest with Jesus

'Take my yoke upon you and learn from me, for I am gentle and humble in heart, and you will find rest for your souls. For my yoke is easy and my burden is light.' (NIV)

As you read this short passage, some of you may be thinking, as I have often thought, 'But I am not finding his yoke easy and his burden light. Life in this world and life as a Christian isn't easy or light.'

But is Jesus promising us a restful, trouble-free life in this world? Or is he promising us soul rest, rest in our spirits in the midst of this world's and this life's difficulties and burdens? I have to conclude that the latter is the case.

And the promise is conditional. It involves being yoked to and learning from Jesus. *The Message* version paraphrases the first part of the verse like this: 'Walk with me and work with me – watch how I do it.'

In Luke 24:36–49, there's the well-known story of a couple of disciples walking and interacting with Jesus. You might like to find a short but very thoughtful and creative theological book on this same passage titled *Moving Towards Emmaus: Hope in a time of uncertainty* by David Smith (SPCK, 2007). The two disciples on the road to Emmaus were in a terrible state before Jesus walked and conversed deeply with them. Their hopes had been dashed and they didn't know what to do, think or believe until they were yoked to and learning from Jesus.

Like them, we are not promised an easy ride through life but, trusting that Jesus is with us, although not physically, we can develop a genuine spiritual relationship with him, talking and listening to him. It is this 'yoke' – suggesting a very close relationship – which can calm and steady our souls and spirits, no matter what is going on in the world and in our lives.

For pondering: 'Learn the unforced rhythms of grace. I won't lay anything heavy or ill-fitting on you. Keep company with me and you'll learn to live freely and lightly' (Matthew 11:29–30, MSG).

JEAN WATSON

SATURDAY 1 FEBRUARY — HEBREWS 4:8–11

Eternal rest?

There remains… a Sabbath-rest for the people of God. (NIV)

This passage is not an easy one to understand but it is generally agreed that the sabbath-rest in this verse is a reference to the final 'rest' in the new heaven and new earth. Rightly understood and not hedged about with man-made prohibitions, the sabbath-rest referred to in the ten commandments was meant to be a very positive, joyful day. So the sabbath-rest for the people of God in the new heaven and new earth will certainly be that and a lot more!

We are not given detailed descriptions of what that time will be like. Jesus speaks in picture language in John 14:1–3 about the rooms in his Father's house which he will prepare for his disciples. And Revelation 21:2–4 tells us that in the 'holy city', free from all evil, God will live with his people and 'there will be no more death or mourning or crying or pain'. Even more: 'What no eye has seen, no ear has heard, and what no human mind has conceived – the things God has prepared for those who love him' (1 Corinthians 2:9).

Eternal rest isn't about doing nothing forever and ever. How boring and uncreative that would be! But it is about being free from all earthly struggles against evil and from all forms of suffering.

It is extremely hard for us to understand what we will be set free *from* and set free *for* because we live in a world of contrasts, of negatives and positives. How can we appreciate light without darkness or joy without experiencing any of its opposites? But can we trust that the God who is at work in this amazing but broken old earth is more than capable of making the new heaven and the new earth perfectly wonderful as well as completely free of all that is evil and unjust?

Talk to God about your hopes and fears in relation to yourself and your loved ones as you think about this eternal rest.

JEAN WATSON

Galatians: set free indeed

Chine McDonald writes:

I grew up in a Christian home and made a decision to become a follower of Christ for myself as a child. I remember those early months and years and the zeal of new-found faith. At various points throughout my life, this faith has grown and been renewed, and I believe I have deepened my relationship with Christ. But I – like most Christians I know – sometimes need a reminder of the faith to which we have been called. Sometimes, the daily grind, the ups and downs of life and the situations presented to us cause us to forget the freedom we have in Christ. The letter to the Galatians is Paul's reminder to the church there of the freedom they have in Christ – a stern telling-off for their straying back to the former things and believing in doctrines that are not the truth of the gospel.

This epistle lays out some of the foundational truths of the Christian faith: justification by faith, equality and freedom. Freedom is one of the values that has been held in high esteem throughout history. Today, the world falsely suggests that things like money, fame and beauty bring us freedom. But we know that true freedom can only be found in Christ.

In the letter – written to be read aloud and shared around the churches in Galatia – Paul admonishes them for thinking that they have to adhere to some of the practices of the Jewish faith, such as circumcision. The wonderful thing about the gospel of Christ is that no extra works are needed. Salvation comes not through anything we have done but through the sacrifice of Christ on the cross. God's ultimate solution to the problem of our sin is the final act. It is finished.

Over the next two weeks, we will explore the letter to the Galatians and be reminded of this truth. It will tell us how freedom in Christ means we are free from the need to boast about anything we have done; it will urge us to not grow weary of doing good; it will highlight the truth that in Christ every one of us is welcomed in, no matter who we are and no matter our background. Every one of us can step into this freedom. He whom the Son sets free is free indeed. What a glorious truth!

SUNDAY 2 FEBRUARY   **GALATIANS 1:1–3**

In it together

Paul, an apostle – sent not from men nor by a man, but by Jesus Christ and God the Father, who raised him from the dead – and all the brothers and sisters with me. (NIV)

From time to time, I suffer from a feeling of inadequacy when I look around at other women. Perhaps I feel they are better mothers, more successful in their careers, kinder, more patient, more beautiful. I have particularly felt that when looking from afar at women whom I would consider my peers or who are in the same life stage as me. A few years ago, however, I made a conscious decision not to suffer from jealousy or feelings of competition or inadequacy, and instead get to know these women.

From there, I began to realise that we are all in this thing called life together. Now, I surround myself with a close group of friends to whom I would previously have compared myself. We meet regularly to eat and to pray together about what is happening in our lives, and share daily conversations and prayer requests – whether it's ahead of difficult meetings, or big personal and family issues. This amazing group of women has helped me through some of the most difficult situations I have encountered and also shared with me in the joys.

The Christian life was never meant to be lived alone. The apostle Paul kicks off his letter to the Galatians telling us that all the brothers and sisters are with him. This is likely to be those he lists in Acts 13, including prophets and teachers, Barnabas and Simeon. Paul's letter to the Galatians is also not intended to be read in isolation, but read aloud, and passed around the churches. Again, this shows how the Christian faith is not a private set of beliefs but a communal message that cannot be lived or understood without others being with us. God never intended us to live this life alone.

Do you have a support network of people you share life with? Ask God to show you today for whom you might provide much-needed support.

                                                                                           CHINE MCDONALD

MONDAY 3 FEBRUARY   **GALATIANS 1:4–10**

No more people-pleasing

Am I now trying to win the approval of human beings, or of God? Or am I trying to please people? If I were still trying to please people, I would not be a servant of Christ. (NIV)

I am a big fan of personality tests. Given the opportunity, when starting a new job and attempting to assess the characters of those with whom I am working, I will be the first to suggest an away day in which we can do some sort of personality test. In answering the introspective questions, we can gain insights into who we are and how we can best work and get along with others. In many of the personality tests I have taken over the years, a strong theme emerges: I am a people-pleaser. People-pleasing is often a trait that is rightly or wrongly associated with women. Many of us grew up in homes where we bore a lot of responsibility and were required to please everybody. Nice girls did not rock the boat.

I know that from a very young age, I was very aware of how others were feeling and saw it as my responsibility to see that everyone was okay – my friends, my sisters, my parents.

If this has been your story, too, then maybe you have taken that need to please everyone into adulthood – into your community, your workplace, your family and your home. I have to confess to often finding myself caring more about what other people think about me than what God thinks. Today's passage is a strong reminder of how wrong it is just to seek the approval of human beings. As followers of Christ made in the image of our creator God, it is in seeking him first and following his command that we can find true freedom, rather than the restrictiveness of pleasing other people.

Lord, help us to be women after your own heart, seeking to please you and not others.

CHINE MCDONALD

TUESDAY 4 FEBRUARY   **GALATIANS 1:21–24**

Bearing witness

I was personally unknown to the churches of Judea that are in Christ. They only heard the report: 'The man who formerly persecuted us is now preaching the faith he once tried to destroy.' And they praised God because of me. (NIV)

I often walk past a man who stands on a bridge on my commute in to work. Every day, he is there as thousands of busy Londoners walk past hurriedly – avoiding his gaze. He stands with a megaphone and a placard. His message is always the same: 'The end is nigh. Repent and turn to God.' In all the years I have walked past this man, I have never seen him speaking to anyone; no one is engaging him in conversation and asking him about the faith he so passionately follows. There is something commendable about having the conviction to do this day in day out; but I do wonder whether he is drawing people closer to God or moving them further away. Prior to his conversion on the road to Damascus, Paul had his own passionate convictions – he thought the Christian faith was abhorrent and so persecuted Christ's followers. The irony of his conversion remains for me one of the most vivid proofs of God's existence.

There is a sentence in today's passage that really struck me: 'And they praised God because of me.' How can we in our daily lives and daily walks draw others closer to God rather than push them further away from him? I have occasionally been told there is something about me that's different. People can't quite seem to put their finger on it. But you and I know that this is the light of Christ shining for others to see. My prayer, however, is that it won't remain for them simple curiosity about a difference, but that through the Holy Spirit I might have the courage to engage them further in conversation; to speak of the goodness and love of God in my life; to tell them that the invitation is open to them, too.

Lord, today give us opportunities to speak of your grace so that others might praise you.

CHINE MCDONALD

WEDNESDAY 5 FEBRUARY   **GALATIANS 2:1–8**

A liberating truth

As for those who were held in high esteem – whatever they were makes no difference to me; God does not show favouritism – they added nothing to my message. (NIV)

Sometimes I feel like an imposter. Over the years, I have found myself in situations where I am the youngest, the only woman, the only person who is not white. In those situations, I feel like I stick out like a sore thumb and feel extremely self-conscious. But alongside those feelings of being the odd one out, often creep the familiar but unwanted feelings of being unworthy. In such situations, I mistakenly listen to the voice in my head, which tells me that I am vastly underqualified to be given these positions of authority. Especially when I am among esteemed individuals, I find myself questioning my worth and my value.

Imposter syndrome is a niggling feeling that eventually you will be found out, and sadly this is how many women feel – whether they are professors, preachers or politicians. If, like me, you have ever felt this way, then take comfort in today's passage. Even if it were true that you are not as accomplished, distinguished or well-qualified as others, it doesn't matter. Paul disregards those 'who were held in high esteem' and reminds us that God does not show favouritism. What a relief. Sometimes we may use the excuse of imposter syndrome – not looking the part or not wanting to step outside our comfort zones – to discount ourselves from stepping in to all that God calls us to. But the wonderful thing is that ordinary women, like you and me, can have extraordinary impact on others in our everyday lives – even when we don't really feel it. God loves us and values us all the time. What a liberating truth that is.

Lord, thank you for the liberating truth that you love us unconditionally – no matter who we are or what we have done.

CHINE MCDONALD

THURSDAY 6 FEBRUARY **GALATIANS 2:9–21**

Facing confrontation

When Cephas came to Antioch, I opposed him to his face, because he stood condemned. (NIV)

It's amazing how quickly a friendship can turn sour when there is disagreement. We all know of people who were once firm friends but who have not spoken for years – perhaps over a disagreement that neither of the parties can agree to reconcile over. Sometimes these disagreements are trivial, but at other times they can be strongly held beliefs, perhaps over theology or doctrine.

Personally, I am one of those people who in the past has avoided conflict at all costs. I could not bear the pain of it and instead did my best to keep the peace – sometimes to the detriment of my own strongly held beliefs or standpoint. But I have learnt over the years that sometimes confronting a friend is good and necessary – especially when it comes to matters of the kingdom.

In today's passage, we see the 'right hand of fellowship' being offered to Paul by Christ's followers including Cephas in verse 9; but just two verses later, Paul opposes Cephas to 'to his face' when he comes to Antioch. How could they so strongly disagree with each other after agreeing to support one another?

For Paul, the confrontation was good and necessary in order to defend the truth of the gospel and its implications for the Christian life. Confrontation when done in a way that treats the other person with love and dignity is good; but, sadly, you may have been on the receiving end of confrontation that turns into conflict because of the way it was handled. Unfortunately, some of us will have had first-hand experience of this within our churches.

In all things, let us remember a song of David: 'How good and pleasant it is when God's people live together in unity!' (Psalm 133:1).

Is there a necessary confrontation that you need to address in your life? Ask God to give you the wisdom and the grace to handle it well.

CHINE MCDONALD

FRIDAY 7 FEBRUARY **GALATIANS 3:1–14**

No longer slaves

He redeemed us in order that the blessing given to Abraham might come to the Gentiles through Christ Jesus, so that by faith we might receive the promise of the Spirit. (NIV)

I often fall into the trap of thinking that slavery is a thing of the past – the transatlantic slave trade was abolished more than 200 years ago, after all. We celebrate the role of influential figures in history such as William Wilberforce, whose Christian faith was his motivation for pushing forward for change.

However, the devastating reality is that there are more slaves today than there were during that time. An estimated 40 million people around the world are victims of human trafficking – bought and sold for labour, sexual exploitation and forced marriage. The numbers are hard to comprehend, but at the heart of these stories are individual lives – real people with hopes and dreams who find themselves in impossible situations. All forms of injustice are abhorrent to God. But there is something about slavery in particular which demonstrates that things are not as God intended, for he is the God of freedom.

When I hear stories of trafficking victims who are freed, thanks to the work of organisations dedicated to ending slavery, I am brought to tears. These stories are wonderful symbols of the grace of God.

Echoing words from Deuteronomy 21:23, Paul writes of the Messiah being hung on a pole – crucified and bearing our sins upon himself. Our redemption through Christ means we are no longer slaves. The wonderful thing is that we do not exchange one form of slavery for another, but instead we are fully redeemed – free indeed – because of Christ, who took the curse for us. He stands in our place and ushers us into true freedom. This promise of true freedom enables us to live each day in the light of it. Remember today that you have been set free from everything – free from the expectation of perfection, free from all addictions, free from the need to please other people. What an amazing gift!

Father God, we thank you for your grace in our lives and the true freedom that comes in following you.

CHINE MCDONALD

SATURDAY 8 FEBRUARY **GALATIANS 3:23–29**

God of welcome

There is neither Jew nor Gentile, neither slave nor free, nor is there male and female, for you are all one in Christ Jesus. If you belong to Christ, then you are Abraham's seed, and heirs according to the promise. (NIV)

When I was four years old, my family moved from Nigeria to the UK, swapping the hustle and bustle of Lagos – Africa's most populous city – for the seemingly quieter streets of south-east London. In the 1980s, there were only a few non-white faces like mine around. I remember realising at a very young age that I stood out – not only was I the tallest in the class for much of my childhood, but there was seldom anyone else who had the same skin colour as me. This difference was most often brought into sharp focus when we were taken on school trips to France. I was not yet a British citizen and so when our class arrived at border control, I would be marched off the bus to have a terrifying conversation with the border officials. In these moments, I felt extremely excluded, alone and unwelcome. Unlike my classmates, whose passports seemed to give them the key to enter any nation they wished, I as an immigrant did not have that same freedom.

Thank God that he is a God of welcome, who ushers us in through his gates with open arms. Thank God that none of us is excluded because of our nationality, race, age, gender or physical ability. We are all children of God not because of anything we have done, but because of the free gift of grace that he has lavished upon us. Today's passage reminds us that we are all equal in the eyes of God and we are all one in Christ Jesus. No distinctions. No favourites. All heirs according to the promise.

Lord, that you welcome everyone with open arms. Thank you for the freedom that comes with accepting your invitation.

CHINE MCDONALD

SUNDAY 9 FEBRUARY   **GALATIANS 4:1–7**

Heirs to the throne

Because you are his sons, God sent the Spirit of his Son into our hearts, the Spirit who calls out, '*Abba*, Father.' So you are no longer a slave, but God's child; and since you are his child, God has made you also an heir. (NIV)

There are not many things that have come close to the joy I felt when finding out I was expecting a child. This long-awaited moment represented a fulfilment of several promises God had made to me over the years that at times I had doubted. My husband and I were overjoyed at this gift, but very conscious that some of our closest friends were yet to experience that same moment.

Now, I come from a family full of women, with nine aunts and two sisters. Girls are my territory. So it hadn't occurred to me that I would ever have a boy. But as I lay on the sonographer's table, this is what she revealed. I was stunned. Today I have a boisterous, curious toddler and could not imagine it any other way. But having a son – and having a child full stop – has enabled me to make more sense of so many passages of scripture that refer to sonship. Having a child forces you to think generationally, about the legacy you will leave behind. As Proverbs 13:22 says: 'A good person leaves an inheritance for their children's children.'

The wonderful thing about the Christian faith, however, as we see in this passage, is that when we enter into God's family, we become heirs to the throne of God above. We are not slaves – not to sin nor to the chains that entangle us – but much-loved *children* of God. In the hustle and bustle of daily life, the to-do lists, the chores and the routines, let us lift our gaze upwards to the one who sees us as his precious, valued, beautiful children.

Thank you, Lord, for our heavenly inheritance. Help us to fix our eyes on you, even in the routine of our daily lives.

CHINE MCDONALD

MONDAY 10 FEBRUARY **GALATIANS 4:8–11**

No turning back

Formerly, when you did not know God, you were slaves to those who by nature are not gods. But now that you know God – or rather are known by God – how is it that you are turning back to those weak and miserable forces? (NIV)

In today's passage, you can sense Paul's growing frustration with the Galatians. This group of people had decided to follow Christ, and were supposed to be living in the light of their new-found freedom in him and following his teachings. After all he had done for them – the great dangers he had risked in establishing the church in Galatia – here they were seemingly right back at square one. Instead of living in freedom, they were behaving as if they wanted to return to the legalism of the former things and the lesser gods they used to worship.

I can understand Paul's frustration. It's easy to see the situation outlined in today's passage and ask what on earth the Galatians were thinking in turning back to those 'weak and miserable forces'. But I wonder whether I, too, sometimes mistakenly fall into the trap of legalism or of putting trust in 'lesser gods'. Walking through any bookshop's self-help section, you will see the range of practices, positive-thinking mantras and therapies to supposedly help fill a perceived hole and make life better – from pregnancy to romantic relationships to tidying up. Some drift into the more obvious categories of 'alternative spiritualities', as society becomes less and less familiar with the idea of God yet more and more filled with existential angst. None of these practices or ways of thinking bring us freedom. They ask us to sign up to modes of behaviour, require us to speak certain words and return to forms of legalism we should have left behind when we became Christians. Paul's stern telling-off is a reminder to us not to look backwards at the former things we used to rely on, but to step forwards into the freedom into which Christ has called us.

Lord, forgive us for the times when we have turned back to the 'former things'. Help us to live in the light of your salvation every day.

CHINE MCDONALD

TUESDAY 11 FEBRUARY   **GALATIANS 4:12–20**

Open arms of welcome

As you know, it was because of an illness that I first preached the gospel to you, and even though my illness was a trial to you, you did not treat me with contempt or scorn. Instead, you welcomed me as if I were an angel of God, as if I were Christ Jesus himself. (NIV)

There are several hints in the New Testament that the apostle Paul suffered from a disability. It is possible that, after being struck blind when he encountered Christ on the road to Damascus, he might have suffered from ongoing eye problems. Commentators offer a number of alternatives.

He talks about this ailment, whatever it was, in today's passage, reminding the Galatians that despite it, they welcomed him into their midst with open arms. In the verses that follow, he asks why they are suddenly treating him so differently because of his truth-telling.

One of the beautiful things about the Christian faith is that everyone is welcome – no matter their race, background, gender or physical ability – as we have already seen in Galatians 3. The Bible is full of examples of those who were in some way not fully able, yet played central roles in God's overall plan. Moses had a speech impediment, Leah had a squint and Gideon suffered from anxiety!

There are many situations in life in which those with physical or mental disabilities are unable to participate freely and fully. Perhaps this is something that you have experience of. Whether these disabilities are seen or unseen, many people are excluded. But this is not the way in the kingdom of God. The church should always be a place in which no person is treated with 'contempt or scorn' and instead every person is completely welcomed and able to fully participate.

Each of us can play a part in demonstrating the radical hospitality of Christ's kingdom within our homes, churches, communities, nations. The way of Christ does not celebrate the rich and the strong, but profoundly celebrates the way of weakness. That is the beauty of our servant king.

Who can you open arms of welcome to today? Consider those in your workplace, local community or church who might be excluded and ask God to show you how you can include them.

CHINE MCDONALD

WEDNESDAY 12 FEBRUARY   **GALATIANS 5:1–6**

Choosing to commit

It is for freedom that Christ has set us free. Stand firm, then, and do not let yourselves be burdened again by a yoke of slavery. (NIV)

Weddings never fail to make me cry. My husband and I recently celebrated our three-year anniversary with a child-free getaway. Over the three years that we have been married, we have attended several weddings – both at home and abroad. It is always wonderful to see two people find love and choose each other, forsaking all others, and to be there to witness their decision to create a life together. They are no longer two, but one. For that moment, all that matters is those two people's love for each other – whatever the future may hold for them.

For some in our society, marriage symbolises the end of a romance rather than the beginning of a love story; it represents shackles rather than freedom. But at a recent wedding I attended, the minister spoke of the fact that while marriage does represent the end of choice, this decision to a complete commitment leads to a profound freedom.

To take another example: someone who decides to take up the violin and become an accomplished violinist has to make a commitment to dedicate many hours working and crafting that skill as the only way that they can eventually find freedom to express themselves through the beauty of musical improvisation. Freedom comes from commitment.

And so it is with the Christian life. Today's passage reminds us again that Christ has set us free. The freedom of following him means that we can say goodbye to the past burdens of slavery. Freedom in Christ is the greatest liberation we can find, because it is in him that we find our heart's desires and the purpose that God has for each of our lives. But we will not find that freedom without daily, personal commitment to him.

Father, help us to commit wholeheartedly to walking in your ways.

CHINE MCDONALD

THURSDAY 13 FEBRUARY GALATIANS 5:13–26

The real thing

But the fruit of the Spirit is love, joy, peace, forbearance, kindness, goodness, faithfulness, gentleness and self-control. Against such things there is no law. (NIV)

My husband and I are in the process of buying a new house – moving out of our tiny flat ever-increasingly filled with baby toys and paraphernalia, and into a real house with stairs and a garden. Alongside the tedium of budgets, conveyancing forms and other house-buying admin comes the joy of designing what the interior might look like. This means weekend trips to home furnishings stores to test out sofas and beds and discuss colour schemes. Walking round these stores, we see pretend set-ups of family homes. Inevitably, somewhere in the showrooms will be fake flowers – and fake bowls of fruit. These wax items bear a striking resemblance to the real things. But, if you were to grab an apple from a fake fruit bowl – as my son might like to do – and bite into it, you would realise very quickly that it is not the real thing.

How do we know when expressions of Christian faith are the real thing? In our performance-driven, social-media obsessed world, it is easy to give the appearance of being an active Christian. Perhaps someone might quote a Bible verse on Twitter or share a highlighted passage on Instagram; but behind the appearance there could be a lack of authenticity.

More dangerous are those who profess to follow Christ yet want to build walls between themselves and others, despite Christ's call to love our neighbour as ourselves. We know from today's familiar passage what real Christian faith looks like. It is marked out by love, joy and peace; it is shown through forbearance, kindness and goodness, always accompanied by faithfulness and full of gentleness and self-control. Those are the marks of the Christian faith that we should each look to possess, knowing that none of it is possible without the helper, the Holy Spirit.

May the fruits of the Spirit be increasingly visible in our daily lives.
CHINE MCDONALD

FRIDAY 14 FEBRUARY **GALATIANS 6:1–10**

Don't give up on the good

Let us not become weary in doing good, for at the proper time we will reap a harvest if we do not give up. Therefore, as we have opportunity, let us do good to all people, especially to those who belong to the family of believers. (NIV)

Sometimes, when I look at the state of the world – the injustice that exists on a global scale – it is easy for me to become overwhelmed. I work within international development and am passionate about standing up for the defenceless. The world is horrendously unequal, with millions of people living in abject poverty, treated with a lack of dignity and facing daily injustices. But this hardship exists not just at a global level, but much closer to home. There are people in our own countries, our own communities, our own streets, who are facing hard times.

The Christian message calls each of us to do good: to feed the hungry, to house the homeless, to treat others as we would want to be treated and love our neighbours as ourselves. But for some of us, life just gets in the way. We are preoccupied with the laundry that needs doing, the endless to-do lists, the key performance indicators and targets at work, the never-ending family crises. But following Christ means that we are compelled to look at the needs of others, not just what is immediately in front of us.

This is a huge daily challenge to me when life feels so full and busy. The reality is, I need to be constantly reminded that I cannot do any of the things God calls me to do in my own strength. That is why I find today's passage so encouraging. It is a rallying call not to get tired of doing good; a reminder not to give up even when things seem much too hard. We are not limited to doing good to others after we have completed all the tasks on our to-do lists. Instead of being overwhelmed, let us celebrate the fact we have a helper who steers us away from self-centredness and enables us to hear God's still small voice, guiding us in the way of goodness.

Lord, in the hustle and bustle of life, may we hear your still small voice.

CHINE MCDONALD

SATURDAY 15 FEBRUARY **GALATIANS 6:11–18**

Picture perfect

May I never boast except in the cross of our Lord Jesus Christ, through which the world has been crucified to me, and I to the world. Neither circumcision nor uncircumcision means anything; what counts is the new creation. (NIV)

'Who knows himself a braggart, let him fear this, for it will come to pass that every braggart shall be found an ass.' These words from Parolles in Shakespeare's *All's Well That Ends Well* are rightly critical of bragging. But the problem is, some of us aren't aware just how much we brag and the effects of our boasting on others.

Many of my generation spend a lot of our time on social media, endlessly scrolling through posts, choosing the perfect photo filter to make ourselves look the best we can possibly look – and crafting the perfect humble-brag: a post that on the face of it looks full of humility but is actually showing off. These often start with 'I'm so honoured to' or 'Feeling incredibly blessed by'. I'm guilty of posting to make myself look good more often than I'd like to admit. I've never shared an Instagram post of my untidy bedroom, the times when I am frustrated with my son, and I rarely share images of myself without make-up or at an unflattering angle.

So many of us present an unrealistic picture of ourselves, which in turn places unrealistic pressures on others. Girls have greater levels of dissatisfaction than boys on social media precisely because of the craving to be valued or seen as beautiful – because this is the picture that we are presenting.

What is it that we boast in? Our jobs, our families, the way we look? My prayer today, like Paul's in today's passage, is that I may never boast except in the cross of Christ. There is a freedom that comes in only boasting in him – the perfect, holy and blameless one: our salvation from sin and our redemption from the darkness that causes us to be slaves to our own image.

Lord, free us from the need to make ourselves look good. May we never boast except in the cross of our Lord Jesus Christ.

CHINE MCDONALD

A window into the heart of God: Revelation 2 and 3

Rachel Turner writes:

Some books in the Bible are an easy read: a straightforward letter between friends, like the book of Philemon. The book of Esther is a quick, engaging tale of bravery and excitement as God saves his people again. Revelation is not usually put on that list of 'easy reading'.

Revelation is a recording of what the apostle John saw and heard from God about the present and the future, while he was a prisoner of Rome on the Greek island of Patmos. It is full of symbolism and fantastic images describing the end of all time and the future of what God will do. There are mind-blowing descriptions of heaven and Jesus, and stunning pictures of angels and of coming wars. Many scholars have written wonderful books for us to wrap our brains around what was written, and there are differing interpretations of what all the images mean. It can be easy to be intimidated by Revelation and many shy away from reading it.

But whenever God speaks, he shows us a part of his heart. Whenever he communicates to us, he reveals something of who he is. By engaging with the book of Revelation, we can see more of God.

At the beginning of John's experience, Jesus gives messages for seven churches in existence at the time. What follows is a series of encouragements and challenges that give us a window into the heart of God for us as individuals and as a united church. For the next two weeks, we are going to be exploring what Jesus said to these churches, and what that window into the heart of God means for us today.

SUNDAY 16 FEBRUARY   **REVELATION 2:1–3**

I know…

I know what you do, how you work hard and never give up. I know you do not put up with the false teachings of evil people. (NCV)

In these two chapters, Jesus starts his messages to each of the seven churches with the words 'I know…' He lays out for each of them what he has seen in the lives of the individuals and the church as a whole. Before he challenges or encourages them, he simply tells them what he has seen in them.

I find that awesome and terrifying.

While I know in my head that God knows and sees everything, in my daily life I can fool myself into thinking I can hide from God. I can keep him at arm's distance, talking to him about safe subjects: my health or concerns about a friend. I can limit the intimacy we have by only deciding to share certain information.

But God is not fooled. He knows. He sees my secret choices and my heart cries of pain. He knows my good behaviours or warped motivations.

On this earth, we often are seeking to be understood by others. It's a slow process of choosing more and more to reveal ourselves, and we hope to be loved, accepted and valued, even in our imperfection. Forming friendships that are open and honest can take years. And yet we often forget that our God, who sees and knows every nook and cranny of our hearts, our thoughts and our characters, is full of love for us. Right now. To be known, the good and bad, is such a vulnerable place to be. It takes boldness to stand exposed before the God of love and holiness. But when we do, we position ourselves to hear the best encouragement and challenge we could ever encounter.

Jesus starts his communications with the churches with the words 'I know…' Are we ready to hear what he sees in us?

Thank you, God, that you see and know all. I open my life to you. Thank you that your love for me is beyond anything I can imagine. I want to hide nothing from you. What do you see in me?

RACHEL TURNER

MONDAY 17 FEBRUARY   **REVELATION 2:1–3**

False teachers

I know you do not put up with the false teachings of evil people. You have tested those who say they are apostles but really are not, and you found they are liars. (NCV)

I can remember it clearly. I was in Year 2, and Mrs Ketchum was teaching spelling. She wrote a word on the board, and I saw that it was spelt wrong. I was shocked – stunned. My teacher was wrong! How was that possible? It had never occurred to me before that moment that teachers were fallible.

It can be incredibly disorienting not to be able to trust what people insist is true. In our society, we are learning more and more to take everything with a pinch of salt. In social media, we are learning we can't trust every news story we see. We are learning to distrust images and magazines online because we know about how the industry manipulates pictures with Photoshop and other programmes. We are learning to question what people present to us.

But do we have the same rigour in our Christian walk? Jesus praises the people in Ephesus for holding Christian teachers to account for what they teach. He encourages the church to put all teaching to the test and to decide for themselves what is right.

It can be easy to spend our Christian lives passively receiving the teaching of others. From Bible notes to podcasts to books and Sunday sermons, there is constant input we can be receiving. It is a gift to benefit from the teaching and wisdom of others. It appears, though, that as we receive, God also wants us to test what we are hearing: to be bold to decide for ourselves, with his wisdom, what teaching to cling to and what to dismiss.

It is part of God's heart for us to grow and mature and to be able to discern what is right as others spiritually feed us.

God, help me to put teaching to the test, so that I can weigh the words of others with wisdom and boldness. Thank you that you promise to guide me into all truth.

RACHEL TURNER

TUESDAY 18 FEBRUARY **REVELATION 2:4–7**

First love

But I have this against you: You have left the love you had in the beginning. So remember where you were before you fell. Change your hearts and do what you did at first. (NCV)

It can be so easy to move from love to obligation. When we first love something or someone, our behaviours follow out of that love. We carve out time for our partners, family or friends and spend hours communicating our love to them. We prioritise them and seek them out. We eat together and make decisions together. But over time, it is easy for those love-based behaviours to accidentally descend into merely obligations and habits, with love somehow missing.

The Ephesus church that Jesus is speaking to here seemed to have lost that love they had at the beginning of their journey with him, and that deeply grieved God's heart. In the passage, he had just praised them for all the good they are doing, and yet despite their good behaviours, he grieved the loss of their love.

If I felt that my husband was merely going through the habits and motions of life together, and yet had lost his love for me, I would be in deep grief too.

Do you remember when you first began to love God? What did it look like?

For me, I can no longer attend every Bible study going, or volunteer in every ministry in the church. I did that at the beginning, but I can't now. However, those things weren't what gave me my love. It was the being in awe of God; the talking to him in the shower; the little ways I saw him in everything and reviewed my day with him in bed.

What did you do at the beginning of your love for God, that kept your heart full of him?

Take a moment to remember your first experience of loving God. Take a few minutes to jot down what you loved about him, and the difference it made to your life.

RACHEL TURNER

WEDNESDAY 19 FEBRUARY   **REVELATION 2:8–11**

The end is the crown

Do not be afraid of what you are about to suffer. I tell you, the devil will put some of you in prison to test you, and you will suffer for ten days. But be faithful, even if you have to die, and I will give you the crown of life. (NCV)

When I first was diagnosed with cancer, I remember desperately wanting to find a promise in scripture that would tell me that God would not let me die from it. I didn't find it.

In this passage, Jesus warns the church of what is to come. He tells them of future suffering, and encourages them to persevere, even to death. He didn't say, 'Don't worry, I can and will rescue you.' He tells them that the future is going to be rough and encourages them to hold tight to him through it, even if it ends in death.

Why do we sometimes assume that life with God is going to be great? Why do we sometimes assume that God's goal for our lives is to be comfortable and pleasant and pain-free? Over and over in scripture, we see a God who declares that he is with us in trouble, rather than always promising to rescue us from it.

The Jesus who was speaking to this church was capable of rescuing them from the coming suffering, but he wasn't going to. Instead, he promised them something much, much better: the crown of life, protection from eternal death. Jesus came to provide for his people the joy of life forever with him, and in his message, he was reminding them of what was before them — not suffering, but life.

There are times when God chooses to rescue us, when he divinely swoops in and saves us, removing obstacles or lifting physical or emotional burdens. I have many stories of this, as I'm sure you do. We know he can do it. But when he doesn't, he strengthens us to cling to the crown of life he lays before us, so that we may always have hope.

God, fill us with your hope. Lift our eyes from our troubles to you, our rescuer. Thank you that you can rescue us now and also give us a crown of life for the future. Push all fear out of our hearts, that we may rest, sure of your love.

RACHEL TURNER

THURSDAY 20 FEBRUARY **REVELATION 2:12–13**

You did not refuse

But you are true to me. You did not refuse to tell about your faith in me even during the time of Antipas, my faithful witness who was killed in your city, where Satan lives. (NCV)

As I watched the car drive away, I felt a wave of regret wash over me. I had just been dropped off by a car rental agency, and the chat in the car hadn't gone well. I didn't want to get sucked into a conversation, so when the woman asked about my work I said, 'I work for a charity', rather than the full truth that I get to spend my days equipping Christian parents to help their kids meet and know the God who loves them. When she asked what I love about the car I rented, I said, 'The sound system is good', instead of the full truth that I sing worship songs at the top of my lungs because it's one of my favourite places to connect with God and heal from tough meetings. It was as if I was refusing to talk about my faith, even in the face of someone who was open to hearing about my life. The next time she dropped me off, I shared those things, and we sat in the car for 45 minutes talking about faith, God, and who he is in difficult times.

We can so often feel that there is a huge expectation and pressure to share our faith with others by forcing faith conversations with people. Yet Jesus didn't praise this church for preaching on street corners. He praised them for not refusing to speak.

A life with God is a beautiful thing that the world needs to hear and see. We don't need to always be sharing the fullness of the four-point gospel plan. Simply speaking of our lives is a powerful display of who God is in the everyday. All it takes is for us not to refuse to speak of it. We can all do that.

God, show me places in my life where I have been refusing to speak. Touch my heart and mouth that I may freely share of who you are in my life.

RACHEL TURNER

FRIDAY 21 FEBRUARY **REVELATION 2:14–17**

Balaam and who?

You have some there who follow the teaching of Balaam. He taught Balak how to cause the people of Israel to sin by eating food offered to idols and by taking part in sexual sins. You also have some who follow the teaching of the Nicolaitans. (NCV)

Whenever I read aloud something like this, I'm just happy to have read the names right rather than understanding what's going on! It always makes me feel so silly, like when someone talks about a movie I've never seen, while everyone around me laughs and talks about it. In real life, we tend to try to escape from those scenarios as quickly as possible, but in scripture, it's quite important to figure out who these people are and why God is talking about them. The people at the time would have known, and so it all made sense to them.

Balaam was a prophet who compromised with the culture around him and allowed it to muddy his call. The Nicolaitans were people who thought that because of Jesus' death and resurrection, we were now free to participate in whatever sin we want; they thought that Jesus gave us freedom from the law and forgiveness for everything. Both groups were saying that a bit of spiritual compromise won't hurt.

Every day, we are offered choices where we can compromise a little bit. Flirt a bit with the delivery guy, commiserate with a colleague about how terrible her boss is, lie about an email. Moment by moment, opportunities arise. Sometimes we go along with it because we think we won't be tempted to anything bigger; sometimes we feel like it's not a big deal; other times we do it because we want to fit in with what is going on around us. Little bit by little bit, we compromise, sometimes without even noticing.

But God notices. He doesn't just say, 'Stop compromising.' He instead challenges what is underneath: 'Change your hearts and lives.'

Compromise is solved not by trying harder, but by having a heart transformation. Where have our hearts become open to compromise?

God, I want to be fully with you, with no compromises. Please remind me of any situations or places where I am compromising, even if I'm not aware of it. Change my heart to be like yours.

RACHEL TURNER

SATURDAY 22 FEBRUARY   **REVELATION 2:18–28**

The faithful

I know what you do. I know about your love, your faith, your service, and your patience. I know that you are doing more now than you did at first. (NCV)

It can be easy when reading this passage to focus on the scary bits. Who is this lady Jezebel? And wow, God sure is serious about sorting her and her followers out! It can become easy to see this passage as primarily about this big issue in the middle, but I wanted to look here at God's beautiful promise on either side of the Jezebel issue.

Before Jesus talks about Jezebel, he graciously affirms the character of some who are at the church. Look again at the passage above.

He recognises their love, faith, service and patience. He sees the sacrifice of their increasing what they were doing before. He sees them. He sees the quiet, everyday faithfulness of his followers.

We can sometimes feel that we want to pour ourselves out to earn God's praise, but here we see a bit of God's heart in the simplicity of what he praises them for and the deep reward for simply continuing in their faithfulness.

Later in the passage, God even restrains himself from adding to their burden, encouraging them to just continue in their loyalty and obedience. In return for their faithfulness, he assures them that he will bless them with power, spiritual gifts, and above all his presence – all for quiet, everyday love, faith, service and patience; for faithful obedience. Amid this massive Jezebel craziness, he sees beyond and calls out in love to the steady few.

Sometimes I feel like I should be better, or flashier, or accomplish something big for God. And then I'm reminded that what God looks for is something different. His heart is good, and he calls his children to be like him, full of love, faith, service, patience and loyalty. Oh, to be more like that!

Thank you, Lord, that you see the hearts of the quiet and steady. God, teach me your ways and meet with me in the quiet places of faithfulness and love.

RACHEL TURNER

SUNDAY 23 FEBRUARY   **REVELATION 3:1–6**

Wake up

Wake up! Strengthen what you have left before it dies completely. I have found that what you are doing is less than what my God wants. So do not forget what you have received and heard. Obey it, and change your hearts and lives. (NCV)

A few months ago, I hid from the world. Ever since I was a teenager, if I wanted time to myself, I would go into the bathroom, turn on the shower, curl on a ball on the floor of the room and cover myself in a towel. Only God had access to me then.

This time, as I lay on the floor, I told God how I was feeling at the end of myself. I was bone tired emotionally and physically, and felt unable to move forward in anything. I felt done. Dry. Void of all life.

As I told God all about it, his still small voice gently came. He reminded me of how he had promised to do my job with me, and how he was present in the middle of my days. He showed me how I had shut joy out of my heart through lack of sleep and an overabundance of worry. He slowly took my burdens off as I handed them to him in my mind, and it was as if I came out of a dream of worry and fog. My soul woke up.

It can be easy to let the secret places of us seem to die. Whether it is our passion for God, our places of peace or joy, our love of scripture or music, life can rob us of the fullness of life Jesus came to give us. Yet God has a simple way out. He reminds us of what we already have been given, of what he has already provided for us, and tells us to cling to it: to his grace and his promises, his closeness and his word.

Have you ever experienced this exhaustion of the soul? Take a moment to ask God to remind you of what he has given you, that you can cling to.

RACHEL TURNER

MONDAY 24 FEBRUARY   **REVELATION 3:7–8**

God opens a door

This is what the One who is holy and true, who holds the key of David, says. When he opens a door, no one can close it. And when he closes it, no one can open it. (NCV)

We have become accustomed to talking about opportunities in our lives in the language of doors. We 'push a door' to see if a new opportunity might be for us. We pray for God to 'open up doors' for people in their ministry and work, and for him to 'close doors' if things aren't right. We tend to use this idea to talk about guidance or finding our next step on our life's journey.

But I just want to take a step back for a second to ponder this. Over and over, we see in scripture a God who isn't constrained by normal human rules like money, reputation, authority or even physics. He provided escape through a body of water for the Israelites, when no one else saw any open route. He raised up Joseph, a prisoner, to lead Egypt in one day. He is the God who can make things happen.

Why, then, am I so fearful sometimes of the fragility of the opportunities that God puts in front of me? I find myself worried that if I don't move fast enough, or if I'm not good enough, doors will close in my face. I push doors that aren't open just to see if I can force them a little bit. I find myself only really knowing if God opened a door after I find myself on the other side of it.

How would our lives be different if we had absolute trust in God's ability to hold open doors that he created, and humbly accept the closed ones in front of us? What greater levels of joy and peace would we live with, supremely confident in God's ability to bring us exactly to where he wants us?

God, forgive me when I worry about doors opening or closing. Fill me with your peace and faith, that I may trust you every step of my journey with you.
RACHEL TURNER

TUESDAY 25 FEBRUARY   **REVELATION 3:10–13**

Inscribed as a citizen

I will make those who win the victory pillars in the temple of my God, and they will never have to leave it. I will write on them the name of my God and the name of the city of my God, the new Jerusalem, that comes down out of heaven from my God. I will also write on them my new name. (NCV)

When we are kids, obedience is something that we must do. It is annoying, but we do it. Our parents asked us to do something, and we gritted our teeth and got on with it. If we didn't, well, we bore the consequences. Sometimes it was effortless and sometimes it took an enormous amount of self-control tinged with a bit of resentment. It is easy to transfer these feelings to the idea of obedience to God. And yet obedience is something designed to bring both us and God great joy. Obedience is how we align our lives with the best God has for us: our greatest path of usefulness to him, a journey of peace and love and purposefulness. It secures our future. Obedience is how we say 'yes' to the great adventures of heart and ministry that God is inviting us into.

The church in Philadelphia held to their faith in the face of persecution, in obedience to God, and just look at the lavish reward God had ready for them. He promises them that he would write on to their very beings his name, make them a part of the structure where he lives and give them the authority and rights of a citizen of his kingdom. All for saying 'yes' to God.

Obedience isn't a breaking of our wills. It's a surrender of them. It's saying, 'God, I belong to you, every bit of me, including my choices. How can I operate as your child today?' God's heart delights in our responding to him like this, and his response, as we see in this passage, is to say, 'Yes, you are mine and I will write my very name upon you.'

Where have we been resisting obeying God and why?

God, I bring to you all of me. I'm sorry where I have clung to my will over yours. Show me any place in my heart where I have been resisting you and help me choose you.

RACHEL TURNER

WEDNESDAY 26 FEBRUARY **REVELATION 3:14–18**

The trap of indifference

You say, 'I am rich, and I have become wealthy and do not need anything.' But you do not know that you are really miserable, pitiful, poor, blind, and naked. (NCV)

I hate lukewarm drinks. I have no idea why. Hot tea? Lovely. Iced tea? Yes please! Room temperature tea? Nope. Wouldn't touch it with a ten-foot pole. Nobody welcomes someone into their home and says, 'Lukewarm drink?' It is gross. Evidently, this dislike for lukewarm drinks goes back millennia.

Jesus is talking to the church in Laodicea and tells them that their hearts towards him are lukewarm, and his feelings about that are like our feelings about a lukewarm drink. We want to spit it out of our mouths!

What disturbs me most about this passage is not that Jesus is repelled by their lukewarmness. It's that they somehow got into this state without really knowing it. They thought they were doing fine. They thought they were great! And yet in reality, it was all empty. But they didn't seem to notice. That scares me. How can people who thought they were on the top of their physical and spiritual game actually be in spiritual poverty and not notice?

God's solution to this seems unusual. He tells them to come buy medicine from him: to purchase gold and clothes and medicine. Not real, earthly ones, but the spiritual wealth of righteousness. The cost is not with human money, but the cost of coming to God and saying, 'I'm all in. All I have is yours. I need your holiness and truth. I want to be clothed in your goodness, pure in all my ways. I need you.'

I don't want to live like a lukewarm cup of tea. Do you?

God, I am sorry where I have allowed my heart to get lukewarm towards you and others. Come stir my heart. I want to say to you that I am fully committed.

RACHEL TURNER

THURSDAY 27 FEBRUARY   **REVELATION 3:19–22**

Consequences

I correct and punish those whom I love. So be eager to do right, and change your hearts and lives. (NCV)

My parents visited my house over Christmas, and my dad and I easily got into old patterns. He is a black belt in a martial art called Aikido, and most of my childhood was spent getting flipped around a mat at the place he trained and practising with him at home. At some point during the Christmas break, Dad and I ended up in the kitchen with him teaching me new and old techniques. I had been pondering this passage for a while, and I was struck by how my father corrected me as he taught me new approaches.

For many of us when we read this passage, we picture God as a slightly grumpy being who watches us make mistake after mistake and doles out punishments in response.

But as my dad taught me new things in the kitchen, it reminded me again of how God responds to us. As I tried techniques that were new to me, I would make repeated mistakes. Each time, my dad would simply say, 'Adjust more here' or, 'Ah, I see what is going wrong; shift your weight this way.' As I responded to his correction, I got better, I understood more, I experienced the delight of getting it right. Correction wasn't a bad thing; it was a necessary process to develop me into the next level of my learning and growth.

I am grateful when God corrects me. Usually when he does, it is because I have been making choices that have been leading me on a path of isolation and stress and sin. His corrections bring me back to peace and grace and joy.

Jesus says that he corrects those he loves. I am so grateful he does.

God, thank you that you don't just leave us to walk our path alone. Thank you that you correct us and grow us that we may live in greater and better freedom in you.

RACHEL TURNER

FRIDAY 28 FEBRUARY   **REVELATION 3:20–22**

Knock, knock

Here I am! I stand at the door and knock. If you hear my voice and open the door, I will come in and eat with you, and you will eat with me. (NCV)

There is something special about a dinner party. I can't quite put my finger on it. Growing up in America, it was much more common to meet friends at a restaurant. I can remember dozens of interesting conversations over the tables at cheap restaurants with my parents' friends, but I have no memory of anyone coming over for a meal.

When I moved to this country 18 years ago, I had to learn a whole new way of making friends. I was baffled. People would invite me into their actual homes and feed me food. It felt so intimate, so welcoming. It was confusing. We had no real relationship, and yet I was so welcomed in that people let me sit in their house and use their toilet. In my childhood, those privileges were reserved only for those closest to us, and usually not that often.

For many of us, we are on a similar journey of relationship with Jesus. We have been happy to do things with him, at arm's distance, out and about in the world or at church events. We have given him his own space with us at designated times and places. And yet, he says that he stands at our door and knocks. He wants to come into our lives and eat with us, to come into the very intimate places of where we live and connect with us.

He won't kick the door down. He won't try to manipulate us into opening the door. He simply knocks. He wants to be part of our ordinary lives: the boring bits of eating, watching television, reading books and driving places. He is knocking, seeking to be with us. Are we bold enough to open the door?

God show me where I am keeping you at arm's length. Let me hear your knocking while I am washing up or relaxing at home, that I may invite you into the ordinary places of my heart and life.

RACHEL TURNER

SATURDAY 29 FEBRUARY REVELATION 2:1, 8, 12, 18; 3:1, 7, 14

The many introductions

The Amen, the faithful and true witness, the ruler of all God has made, says this. (NCV)

I never feel I do introductions well. 'Hello! My name is Rachel Turner, and I'm a musical-loving, history-reading, loud introvert who feels called to encourage people. And I wear odd socks.' It's really hard to try to summarise yourself into a short and snappy introduction. It somehow never really feels comprehensive enough. It feels false or incomplete.

And I'm just an ordinary human: I can't imagine the challenge God has of trying to put into limited human words the fullness of himself. But all through these passages that we have been reading over the last two weeks, God has continually been introducing himself. In every one of the letters to the seven churches, he introduces himself differently.

The One who holds the seven stars in his right hand and walks among the seven golden lampstands. The One who is the First and the Last, who died and came to life again. The One who has the sharp, double-edged sword, who has eyes that blaze like fire and feet like shining bronze. The One who has the seven spirits and the seven stars. The One who is holy and true, who holds the key of David. The faithful and true witness. The ruler of all God has made.

When I read that list, I am in awe. The God who loves us is mighty and beyond understanding. He is impossible to fully comprehend, and yet this all-powerful and perfect being loves us. Unworthy as we are, he corrects us, guides us, knocks on our doors seeking to come in. And to ensure we know, he commissioned a man to send letters to some churches to tell them so. What a God we serve.

God, thank you for your determination to reveal yourself to us, that we may know you and walk with you.

RACHEL TURNER

Thirsty for God: Book 2 of the Psalms

Nell Goddard writes:

I'm willing to bet you know what it's like to be thirsty. It's a deep need, a human desire. It can come on slowly during a workout or strike you all of a sudden at the end of a busy day when you just haven't found the time to stop and pour yourself a glass of water.

We know what it's like to be thirsty – for water, at least. But what does it mean to be thirsty for God? It's a question that seems to come in two parts: 'What does it mean to be thirsty?' and 'Who is this God after whom we are thirsting?'

We've touched on the first question already, but let's deal with the second question first.

I don't know about you, but I occasionally find that 'God' can become somewhat of an abstract, as I read about and think about and pray to him, but sometimes fail to actually spend time learning about *who* he is – his character, his heart, his desires.

I set myself a challenge: discover what the psalms say about who God is. Which characteristics of God do these psalms reflect, declare, desire, and celebrate?

I found my answer(s). God is a God of salvation, a God of justice, one who offers forgiveness, who is worthy of praise. He is a refuge, one who offers us true rest.

But how does that tie in with our initial idea of thirst? Thirst seems an unpleasant predicament, an inconvenience, a problem to be solved.

So what if, when we consider what it means to be thirsty for God, we thought not of a desire for our thirst to be quenched, temporarily satisfied (so that we can carry on with lives as before), but instead a desire which, when fulfilled, alters our lives entirely? A reorientation, a gear-shift, a direction change.

As we journey together through the psalms over the next seven days, my prayer is this: may we thirst and be satisfied. May we discover the deep well of living water, hidden in the character of our infinite creator God. May our thirst for him be constant so we find within us a desire to drink forever more.

SUNDAY 1 MARCH   **PSALM 42**

Thirsty for God

As the deer pants for streams of water, so my soul pants for you, my God. My soul thirsts for God, for the living God. When can I go and meet with God?… Why, my soul, are you downcast? Why so disturbed within me? Put your hope in God, for I will yet praise him, my Saviour and my God. (NIV)

Do you ever talk to yourself? I have a friend who likes to debrief the day with himself, aloud. It's a little weird, but you get used to it after a while.

Talking to yourself might be seen as the habit only of eccentrics nowadays, but this psalm is someone engaging in dialogue with their soul.

It begins, however, with the psalmist's desire to meet with God – a lament, a deep longing for the life-giving God. God is presented as being as integral to the psalmist's survival as water is to the life of a parched animal. It is likely that the psalmist wished to go to the temple to meet with God but was unable to do so. And so, this psalm is a psalm of struggle, of longing, of grief at feeling cut off from God's presence.

Do you ever feel cut off from God? Perhaps you are unable to attend church because of health reasons, or circumstances have made God feel far away.

Whatever your situation, this psalm offers a suggestion: talk to yourself. Encourage yourself. You might feel a little daft, but words spoken aloud have power and weight. So, today, why not take a leaf out of the psalmist's book and exhort your very soul. Remind yourself of the future hope: 'Yet I will praise him.' Instruct yourself: 'Put your hope in God.' And talk to him! Aloud?

This psalm reminds us that no matter how we *feel*, there is still hope to be found when we bank on God. Yet we will praise him – no matter the situation. We too can encourage our souls, talk to ourselves, encourage our weary minds and hearts, safe in the knowledge that he is our Saviour and our God.

God, sometimes I feel that meeting with you is a distant dream. Teach me to speak truth to my soul and to put my hope in you nonetheless, safe in the knowledge that 'yet I will praise you, my Saviour and my God'.

NELL GODDARD

MONDAY 2 MARCH   **PSALM 51:1–12**

Thirsty for forgiveness

Have mercy on me, O God, according to your unfailing love; according to your great compassion blot out all my transgressions. Wash away all my iniquity and cleanse me from my sin… Hide your face from my sins and blot out all my iniquity. (NIV)

Have you ever done something and immediately regretted it? Whether it was an accident or a deliberate choice, sometimes we act and are filled with guilt right afterwards. We just know, deep within ourselves, that we will have no rest until we make it right with the one we have wronged.

That is where this psalm begins. David has done wrong, and he is seeking after God for forgiveness. But this isn't just a quick 'I'm sorry' psalm. This psalm reflects a deep intimacy with God, as David seeks an inner transformation.

Three different words are used for David's wrongdoing: transgressions, iniquity and sin. 'Transgression' is a rebellion against God's commands; 'Iniquity' is crookedness or perversion, and 'sin' is missing a mark (think of an arrow not hitting its target). Each of these words requires action from God: transgressions must be blotted out, iniquity washed away and sin cleansed.

David is desperate for forgiveness. He has realised the depths of his brokenness and how it has damaged his relationship with God. 'Hide your face from my sins,' he requests. In a book full of psalms pleading for God to turn his face *towards* the psalmist, this is stark.

When was the last time you sought such forgiveness from God? The last time you were so utterly ashamed of yourself and your wrongdoing that you could not bear the idea of God even looking at you? Whether it was transgression, iniquity or sin – or a combination of all three – consider using this psalm as a prayer.

As you pray it, stand firm in the knowledge that 'if we confess our sins, he is faithful and just and will forgive us our sin and purify us from all unrighteousness' (1 John 1:9).

'According to your great compassion blot out my transgressions.' Thank you, Father, that you are compassionate, faithful and kind, and always more willing to forgive than we are to repent. Teach me to seek true forgiveness.

NELL GODDARD

TUESDAY 3 MARCH   **PSALM 54**

Thirsty for salvation

Save me, O God, by your name; vindicate me by your might. Hear my prayer, O God; listen to the words of my mouth… Surely God is my help; the Lord is the one who sustains me. (NIV)

I hit a pheasant with my car when driving alone to preach somewhere. The pheasant got stuck in my car grille, and I panicked. The first thing I did was ring my dad. 'Help me!' I said.

Why did I ring my dad? I felt helpless and I didn't know what to do (turns out no one briefs you for a 'pheasant stuck in car grille' situation). I trusted my dad to help me and I knew that, even if he wasn't physically with me, he (and my mum) would know what to do.

Our first port of call in situations where we feel helpless is to turn to someone we trust – whether they're physically with us or not. Whether that's a family member, a friend, or a professional, we know who we need to talk to.

The psalmist here was the same; stuck in a situation of injustice, he turns to God: 'Save me, O God.' He is longing – desperate, in fact – for salvation.

How often is God your first port of call when you are feeling helpless? When did you last cry out to God to save you? Maybe you've never been in a situation where you felt trapped and helpless… or maybe you've been in more than you can count.

It can be easy to try and solve things ourselves, or to turn to people around us for practical help. But to turn to God for salvation, for help, is to acknowledge God as one who can bring justice, who is all-powerful to help us in our time of need: 'Surely God is my help, the Lord is the one who sustains me.'

Think of someone you know currently in a seemingly impossible situation. Use this psalm as a prayer for them, and then get in contact to see if you can help them in any way.

NELL GODDARD

WEDNESDAY 4 MARCH PSALM 61

Thirsty for refuge

Hear my cry, O God; listen to my prayer. From the ends of the earth I call to you, I call as my heart grows faint; lead me to the rock that is higher than I… I long to dwell in your tent for ever and take refuge in the shelter of your wings. (NIV)

What do you do when you're feeling overwhelmed? Panic? Power down? Eat? Shop? Hide away from everyone? Knuckle down and try to get stuff done? Become paralysed by the amount you have to cope with, and therefore feel unable to do anything?

We all feel overwhelmed sometimes – whether it's work pressures, relationship trouble, health concerns, emotional burdens, or finding ourselves in dire financial straits… Things pile up and suddenly, sometimes before we've even really registered what's going on, we feel as if we are drowning under worries, tasks and responsibilities.

This psalm is a psalm of trust and confidence, beginning with a cry to God. We can cry out to God in every circumstance and situation – even, it says, 'as my heart grows faint' or, in the Amplified Bible, 'when my heart is overwhelmed and weak'. And this isn't just at the temple, where God had promised to be – the psalmist is petitioning God 'from the ends of the earth'. Even when we feel far from God, we can cry out to him.

If I'm honest, when I feel overwhelmed, turning to God isn't often my first reaction. As a fiercely independent problem-solver, I tend to think I just need to work a little harder, put a bit more time in, sacrifice something 'less' important… and then I'll be able to get back in control of both the situations and my emotions.

But this psalm reminds us that, no matter what we feel overwhelmed by, and whether or not we feel able to 'fix' it ourselves, our first port of call should always be God. When we feel overwhelmed, as and when our 'heart grows faint', we must seek to 'take refuge in the shelter of [his] wings'.

Lord, when I am feeling overwhelmed, teach me to seek first your refuge and your shelter, no matter the storms that surround.

NELL GODDARD

THURSDAY 5 MARCH   **PSALM 62**

Thirsty for rest

Truly my soul finds rest in God; my salvation comes from him… Yes, my soul, find rest in God; my hope comes from him. Truly he is my rock and my salvation, he is my fortress, I shall not be shaken. My salvation and my honour depend on God; he is my mighty rock, my refuge. (NIV)

'You have made us for yourself, O Lord, and our heart is restless until it rests in you.'

In this passage of the *Confessions*, St Augustine was talking about our continuous human effort for fulfilment and how we will only find true satisfaction in God. But even when we have sought and been found by our creator God, we still battle with a very human need for true, deep rest.

So, how good are you at resting? Are you a Netflix binge-watcher, or an activity-holiday kind of person? If you have a young family or a busy job, or if you struggle with chronic illness, you might feel that you rarely get any real rest.

The opening verse of this psalm seems to suggest that the psalmist has it sorted – 'Truly my soul finds rest in God.' But this isn't a statement of fact or the psalmist declaring a reality. Instead, it should be read as an exhortation to one's self. The emphasis in the original text isn't on the rest itself but on God, the source of the rest.

When you're worn out, run down and exhausted, where do you turn? How often do you go first to God for rest? When we long for rest, it can be so easy to go straight to things that distract our brain – TV, books, activities. And those are good things… but, this psalm suggests, they are not true 'rest'. True rest, it says, is found in God. He does not just offer respite from the world's busyness but when we seek our rest in God, we find salvation, hope and honour there too. God is described as a 'rock', a 'fortress' and a 'refuge'.

When we turn to God as our resting place, we find that his character encompasses all that we have ever needed – and more.

Father, teach me to seek my rest in you and you alone.

NELL GODDARD

FRIDAY 6 MARCH PSALM 66

Thirsty to praise

Shout for joy to God, all the earth! Sing the glory of his name; make his praise glorious… Come and see what God has done, his awesome deeds for mankind! He turned the sea into dry land, they passed through the waters on foot – come, let us rejoice in him. (NIV)

Have you ever been so excited you thought you could burst? Maybe you had some particularly good news, or planned a surprise for a loved one that you just *can't wait* to tell them about. This is the psalm of someone who cannot contain their joy and thanksgiving.

It begins with universal praise – 'shout for joy to God, all the earth!' (v. 1) – then moves into national praise – 'come and see what God has done, his awesome deeds for all mankind!' (v. 5) – until finally there is personal praise: 'come and hear, all you who fear God; let me tell you what he has done' (v. 16).

This psalm is about Yahweh himself, the one true God. As the psalmist considers all that God has done for him and his people, he is led to worship. As a part of this worship, he invites those who are listening – and the world at large – to come and behold what God has done and how he has blessed his people.

It is so easy to get caught up in the monotony of everyday life – eat, work, tweet, sleep, repeat – and forget to dwell on how God has intervened in our lives to bring us to the point at which we currently find ourselves, and how he's blessing us here as well.

We are so good at asking for prayer when things go wrong. But what if we made a habit of asking others to join us in thanksgiving as well? We can praise him for tangible things in our daily lives as well as big grand sweeping things that immediately lead us to awe and worship. Point those around you to God – with declarations of his goodness in your life and theirs.

Come, let us rejoice in him!

Take some time today to share a way that God has worked in your life recently, and invite fellow believers – family, friends, small group members – to join you in praising God for it.

NELL GODDARD

SATURDAY 7 MARCH   **PSALM 72**

Thirsty for justice from earthly rulers

Endow the king with your justice, O God, the royal son with your righteousness. May he judge your people in righteousness, your afflicted ones with justice. (NIV)

When I was growing up, we had a guy in our church who would insist on praying for politicians and royalty whenever he did intercessions… except he would always get their names wrong. Praying for 'Duncan Cameron' always gave me the giggles, and I struggled to concentrate on anything else.

But in the midst of my laughter, I was missing something important: we were praying for our leaders. It can be so easy to complain and disparage our political situation and those who are leading us through it… but this psalm instructs us otherwise.

Pray for your leaders – pray that they would be endowed with justice. 'That's not fair!' is the cry of the disgruntled child, but it points to a deep-seated desire for justice and fairness that we all possess and that comes from God. This psalm is a prayer that the king – the leader – would bring justice to those who need it and prosperity to the land he rules.

What would it look like for us to pray this over our Prime Minister, our governments, our monarchs? To pray it not only for our country, but for countries around the world? What might change if we committed to pray that our leaders would be 'endowed with justice'?

This psalm – along with the rest of the Bible – shows us that God has a special concern for the poor, the weak and those who have nothing. As disciples of Jesus, we are called to the same concern and called to pray that those who lead would be given the same desire for righteousness and justice.

So whether you know the names of our leaders or not, commit to praying that in every situation they would seek justice for those who need it.

Today, pray for the leaders not only of this country, but of the world as well. Ask God that those in power would be endowed with his justice, and that their decisions would ultimately benefit the weak and the vulnerable.

NELL GODDARD

Visions and visitations

Sara Batts writes:

For the next two weeks, our readings are on the theme of 'visions and visitations': the times when God breaks through into human experience and we are given glimpses of heaven through dreams, angels and prophets. I think these passages help us understand more about the nature and character of God.

We will follow the story from Genesis and the fall, through Israel's history, to the work of the early church after Jesus' death and resurrection. This broad outline helps us fit the individual visions and visitations into the wider narrative of God's work. Many stories in the fortnight to come will be very familiar to us – Moses, Daniel, Mary; the transfiguration and the Damascus road. I have also included a few that might be less well-known, or have highlighted a vision that is secondary to a story we know well. There are interesting links to be seen between some of the readings. We spend four days with Acts, hopefully inspiring us to share the good news of Christ as we approach Easter.

It's tempting to skip the weird imagery in the prophecies that can be hard to understand. It's easy to make angels into cutesy ornaments instead of terrifying instruments of God's word. It's challenging to wait on the guidance of the Holy Spirit and to feel frustrated when we long for clear instructions from our heavenly Father.

The apocalyptic, the astounding and the overwhelming descriptions also help prevent us from creating God in our own image. We are reminded that God is outside of our time, our human boundaries and understanding. In Lent, as we continue to prepare for the momentous events of Good Friday and Easter Sunday, these passages can help us truly appreciate the power and magnificence of God. They take us out of the ordinary. They help us understand the awesomeness of God.

Wherever we are in our journey and relationship with God, I believe there are lessons we can learn to help us find heaven breaking through into our day-to-day ordinary lives. In our troubled and uncertain times, we can find reassurance that God does still guide us, that God does still put the people in our path that we need – even if not necessarily via traffic-stopping, donkey-talking angels!

SUNDAY 8 MARCH   **GENESIS 3:1–13**

Hiding from the presence of God

They heard the sound of the Lord God walking in the garden at the time of the evening breeze, and the man and his wife hid themselves from the presence of the Lord God among the trees of the garden. (NRSV)

We begin with the man and woman hiding from God's presence. God was walking in his beautiful garden, seeking his creations – and they were ashamed. They could not bear to be in his presence. You might think it's cheating, beginning with something that isn't necessarily either a visit or a visitation – but I wanted to explore how the story of the fall begins the story of our separation from God.

If sin was not in the world – if our relationship with God was as perfect as he had intended – then we might be able to enjoy the kind of easy companionship of a stroll in a beautiful garden that we imagine in Genesis 3. We could live in the security of being always in his tangible presence; we could live with the wonder of worshipping our creator. What woe is ours that we have lost this!

Sin separates us from God. Our best intentions are thwarted by the very nature of being a fallible human. Did you begin Lent with good intentions of fasting and prayer? You wouldn't be alone if you struggled with strict resolutions after only a few days. Guilt and shame can prevent us from seeking God – fearing judgement not forgiveness, we hide ourselves away.

Lent is the time when we can fling open the dusty cupboards of our souls and have a good clear-out. We can name the things we are ashamed of, and be assured of God's forgiveness. It takes courage to do that; we might much prefer to keep things hidden. I really would not want to meet God face-to-face in my worst moods. Yet, we know that God is overjoyed when we seek him. And we know that he understands what it is to be human. There is no need to hide.

'In him we have redemption through his blood, the forgiveness of our trespasses, according to the riches of his grace that he lavished on us' (Ephesians 1:7–8).

SARA BATTS

MONDAY 9 MARCH   **GENESIS 28:10–22**

Dreaming of the presence of God

Then Jacob woke from his sleep and said, 'Surely the Lord is in this place – and I did not know it!' (NRSV)

I recently climbed Jacob's Ladder in the Peak District. It's named after its creator, but the experience certainly brought biblical Jacob to mind. Halfway, thick fog began to descend – so I felt I was ascending into the heavens, despite feeling somewhat lonely in the fog.

I wonder if Jacob was lonely too as he made his way towards Haran. Was he weighed down by a guilty conscience? We meet him as he flees his father Isaac's household. If you're not familiar with the story of Esau and Jacob, it's worth reading Genesis 27 for a soap opera-worthy tale of intrigue and deceit.

Jacob has a vision of angels ascending and descending a ladder from earth to heaven. He hears the voice of God speak reassuring promises. I wonder if you, like me, would long to have this kind of unequivocal experience? I wonder too, whether Jacob's cry is one you have been privileged to echo: 'Surely the Lord is in this place – and I did not know it!'

Have you heard the expression 'a thin place?' It's a Celtic Christian idea that there are places where the gap between heaven and earth is narrowed. It might be somewhere obviously religious – a cathedral, a tiny church – or it might be Liverpool Street station or a motorway service area. What matters is that it is a place where we expect to encounter God.

Do you have a 'thin place?' Are you able, during Lent, to spend time there? And if you haven't a special place, can you spend time in prayer in different places? With new images? Could you look for a space or an image that would nurture your prayer and spirit in future? My prayer is that you will be able to say, 'Surely, the Lord is in this place.'

Father God, help me seek you anew today. Help me be attuned to the places that will inspire me to wait on you.

SARA BATTS

TUESDAY 10 MARCH   **EXODUS 3:1–15**

Standing in the presence of God

'Remove the sandals from your feet, for the place on which you are standing is holy ground.' (NRSV)

Yesterday we looked at the idea of thin places, where we feel close to God. Today we're looking at one of the most well-known instances – Horeb, where Moses encounters God in the burning bush. We have skipped ahead, past the death of Jacob's son Joseph, to the time when the Israelites were enslaved, rather than welcome, in Egypt.

'I must turn aside and look at this great sight,' says Moses.

How often have I missed something amazing because I was so set on a particular task, path or frame of mind? I think that Moses reminds us that we do have to turn aside sometimes to truly notice the extraordinary. That reminder is particularly pertinent in Lent. If we are seeking God, but continue as normal with our daily lives, will we create the space he can fill?

I love and hate contemplative prayer in equal measure. Being open, being wordless and being expectant before God can be an amazing experience. Sitting still is almost always the exact opposite of what I want to do at any given time. Yet I know that when I have found time to turn away from the pressure of busyness, I feel both mentally and spiritually refreshed. Practising mindfulness – being fully aware of the present moment – works for many. Both require us to stop ourselves in our tracks and pay attention to what is happening around us – which is exactly what Moses did.

And he found God, waiting for him, waiting to trust him with the task of leading the Israelites to freedom. He found God ready to reveal his purpose – and his most holy name.

Whoever we are, a response to today's reading might be to deliberately choose to turn aside and focus on God. He is with us; our own home can be holy ground.

SARA BATTS

WEDNESDAY 11 MARCH **NUMBERS 22:22–35**

Unlikely messenger of God

Then the Lord opened the eyes of Balaam, and he saw the angel of the Lord standing in the road, with his drawn sword in his hand; and he bowed down, falling on his face. (NRSV)

I couldn't resist including this story in our collection. It is amusing, and a little whimsical – and helps us understand an important point about God's revelation.

Led by Moses, the Israelites are nearing the end of their 40 years' wandering. Balak, King of Moab, is afraid he will be defeated by the Israelites and summons Balaam to curse them. God speaks to Balaam, at first telling him not to go, then telling him he can go but to only speak the words God gives him. En route, God seems to change his mind and sends an angel to intercept Balaam.

Only the donkey can see the angel – and very sensibly it attempts to avoid him. This happens three times until 'the Lord opened the mouth of the donkey' and rebukes Balaam for striking him.

Numbers only records Balaam's answer. It doesn't tell us if he was at all surprised by a talking donkey! When I try to imagine this scene, the humour does rather outweigh the awe of the appearing angel. My sympathies lie with the donkey – and I find myself wondering what else we would hear if our animals could speak.

There are two serious points that we can take from this passage. Firstly, that we can't always see what others see. Understanding someone else's point of view, being able to interpret events as they do – not just from our own perspective – is one of the fundamental parts of loving our neighbour. And secondly, that God will use unlikely messengers to help us understand what is going on. I'm not expecting a talking donkey any time soon, but I might be more attuned to the voices of people I don't always hear – because they may well be able to tell me something important that I cannot understand by myself.

Thank you, God, for the gift of humour. Thank you for the many ways in which your message to us is presented. Help me to truly listen to those around me so that I may hear and understand your word.

SARA BATTS

THURSDAY 12 MARCH 1 KINGS 3:3–28

Wisdom gives life

At Gibeon the Lord appeared to Solomon in a dream by night; and God said, 'Ask what I should give you.' (NRSV)

Who wouldn't want to be known for their wisdom? As my secondary school motto taken from Ecclesiastes 7 says, 'Wisdom giveth life.' What decisions we might revisit with the wisdom of hindsight!

We have fast-forwarded again. The Israelites have been settled for generations. David's reign has ended; Solomon's is just beginning. He summons all in leadership to the temple of the Lord and gives a large burnt offering. We read that God later appears to Solomon and asks what God should give to him. Solomon famously asks for the wisdom and knowledge for which he becomes renowned.

Wasn't he already wise to know that he needed wisdom? Solomon acknowledged that he was 'only a little child' who did not know 'how to go out or come in'. Solomon knew himself. Solomon knew what he lacked; and he had the humility to ask for it. What might we ask for? I think it only proves we're human if we sometimes wish for more power or influence, or an end to financial or relationship troubles. Those are not inherently wrong things to ask for – but Solomon shows us the way that God would have us be.

As I write, I am in the midst of a dilemma over a broken working relationship. I long for clear-cut judgement over how to proceed; how to bring two people together who seem so very far apart in their perceptions of a wrongdoing. Messy human relationships don't lend themselves to neat solutions – which can be very frustrating. Solomon teaches us that humility and an understanding of our own limitations leads to trusting in God. And trusting in God is often all we can do.

'Take my instruction instead of silver, and knowledge rather than choice gold; for wisdom is better than jewels, and all that you may desire cannot compare with her' (Proverbs 8:10–11).

SARA BATTS

FRIDAY 13 MARCH ISAIAH 6

Awesome warnings

In the year that King Uzziah died, I saw the Lord sitting on a throne, high and lofty; and the hem of his robe filled the temple. (NRSV)

Sometimes, I think we focus more on the encouraging and inspiring call to prophesy than on the actual message to be spoken. 'Send me' – but Isaiah has a terrible warning to deliver in the face of Israel's rejection of God.

Israel has repeatedly broken the covenant with God established at Sinai. Years earlier, at the dedication of the temple, Solomon had reminded the people of the covenant (1 Kings 8), but that didn't bring about long-term change in the attitude of the people. Now Isaiah must warn the people of the consequences of their actions.

Isaiah sees the full glory of the Lord and is afraid. Six-winged seraphs; smoke; shaking thresholds: that would be awesome enough without the Lord, high and lofty, to complete the terror. Yet the question and answer in verse 8 is, I think, one of the most inspiring verses in the prophetic literature.

'Here I am, send me!' Can we honestly say that to the Lord without qualification? Send me: but to people I understand. Send me: but I don't want to be worse off financially. Send me: but not yet. Those are all reactions I have had!

Prophets deliver unpopular messages. Prophets have to tell people to change their ways, mend their behaviour, repent of their sin. In our individualistic, consumer-driven society, much of what I preach will be unpopular. Caring for creation might mean making life inconvenient. The need to love; to forgive; to love justice and to show mercy – these are uncomfortable things to have to do. Replicating the radical love of Jesus for the marginalised might make us unpopular. Questioning the structures that marginalise people definitely will! Are you ready to answer the call?

'And what does the Lord require of you but to do justice, and to love kindness, and to walk humbly with your God?' (Micah 6:8).

SARA BATTS

SATURDAY 14 MARCH   **EZEKIEL 1**

Awesome glory

Like the bow in a cloud on a rainy day, such was the appearance of the splendour all round. This was the appearance of the likeness of the glory of the Lord. (NRSV)

What is your reaction to this reading? Do you try to imagine the creatures, the wheel and the fire? Or do you skip hurriedly over it, more interested in the words from God in the next chapter than the fantastic backdrop this vision provides?

I think I would be terrified if I were caught up in this kind of vision. It's hot, busy and noisy. It is unlike anything we have ever seen. No wonder the prophet falls on his face. It's prophecy from the time of exile, after the catastrophe Isaiah was warning of has come about.

Note how the passage uses the word 'like': 'something like four living creatures' (v. 5). It sounds to me as if the writer does not have the words to record what he has seen. It sounds as if the writer is witnessing a vision so far out of his normal experience that approximation is the best he can do. The 'appearance of the likeness of the glory of the Lord' is two descriptions removed from the reality. Whether we can imagine this scene or not, it is mind-boggling.

This vision helps me remember that God truly is awesome! He is beyond description. When I pray to God, it is sometimes easy to forget that. I know my prayers are heard, and somehow that domesticates God to my level as if I were chatting with a friend. Yes, the risen Jesus is a friend. Yes, we can talk to God however and whenever we want. But let's not forget he is the eternal creator of the universe. Remembering that God is indescribably more than we can imagine helps me put God into true perspective. If I doubt his power, such visions remind me of his limitlessness. He is majestic and awesome: yet he cares about me, too.

Lord God, how glorious is your majesty! Thank you that in your infinite power you still number the hairs on my head. Thank you that I can call you 'Father'.

SARA BATTS

SUNDAY 15 MARCH   **DANIEL 7:1–14**

Awesome judgement

Daniel said: 'In my vision at night I looked, and there before me were the four winds of heaven churning up the great sea. Four great beasts, each different from the others, came up out of the sea.' (NIV)

Stories from Daniel are Sunday school favourites: Daniel in the lions' den; Shadrach, Meshach and Abednego in the fiery furnace. These great stories of God's power are well known. Yet the second half of the book of Daniel sits in contrast to these stirring tales. Daniel 7 begins to tell of terrifying visions of beasts and judgements. This is apocalyptic stuff!

Daniel, like Ezekiel, is a book of the exile. One interpretation says the beasts represent Babylon, Persia and the Greek and Roman empires, thus reflecting the contemporary political landscape. Exile – deportation to Babylon – was catastrophic for the Jewish people. The land at the heart of their covenant with God was gone. The warnings of Isaiah and others had gone unheeded.

The historical interpretation isn't the only way to understand this passage, though. Daniel gives us a vision that can encompass all human history. It's no wonder, then, that symbolism is needed to try to grasp the concepts, just like in Ezekiel. It is not necessary to find exact matches of symbol and history; it is enough to recognise that there are certain constancies – not least the final triumph of God's power.

The vision shows judgement on the beasts – death and powerlessness. The Ancient of Days, the One who has existed since before time, is enthroned. God is, after all, still sovereign.

Then there is the coming of 'one like a son of man'. He is from heaven, but fully related to humanity. When we meet the phrase 'Son of Man' in the gospels, it is on Jesus' lips – and when he is talking about his future suffering (Mark 14:62). Daniel points forward to the suffering and persecution; Jesus reminds us that in this vision Daniel prefigures the future hope of God's glory.

What if the four beasts were our own fears and inner demons – the things that thwart our desire to stay close to God and keep us in exile? Let us not be afraid of judgement, but remember our redemption in Christ.

SARA BATTS

MONDAY 16 MARCH   **LUKE 1:26–38**

Awesome favour

Then Mary said, 'Here am I, the servant of the Lord; let it be with me according to your word.' Then the angel departed from her. (NRSV)

This might be the most well-known angelic appearance in the Bible. Familiar from nativity plays, Gabriel's visit has been represented countless times in art, music and poetry.

Mary was much perplexed – thoroughly shaken or troubled, according to other translations. The angel Gabriel tells her not to be afraid – although she doesn't appear to be as terrified as other recipients of visits from angels have been. She questions Gabriel in an entirely rational manner, continuing the tradition of Moses in being upfront about her misgivings. In fact, people have linked the burning bush and the annunciation since the fourth century, though not for the similarity of response as we might think. Instead, the burning bush was not consumed and so was seen as prefiguring Mary's virginity remaining intact.

Mary's response, in words that echo those in Isaiah 6, is simple: 'Here am I, the servant of the Lord.' Was it a quiet, wondering whisper? Did she proclaim it loudly?

Those words have shaped responses women have made to the Lord for centuries since: words that keep us secure in our sense of calling to serve him and others. Mary is a powerful figure showing the power of a 'yes'.

I believe that Mary must always have had a choice in her response to the visit from Gabriel – otherwise our free will, our ability to choose or reject God, is compromised.

Mary, the mother of God. Mary, the one through whom the incarnation becomes a reality. Heaven touches earth; God breaks into our world. Gabriel reminds us that 'nothing will be impossible with God'. How often do we remember this?

Lord God, with the example of Mary before me, help me serve you today. Help me to remember that nothing is impossible for you.

SARA BATTS

TUESDAY 17 MARCH   **MATTHEW 17:1–8**

Awesome ancestors

Then Peter said to Jesus, 'Lord, it is good for us to be here; if you wish, I will make three dwellings here, one for you, one for Moses, and one for Elijah.' (NRSV)

A few years ago, I visited Innsbruck and (taking a cable car!) stood 2,256 metres up at the top of Hafelekar, in the Karwendel range. It was my first time in real mountains, and it was breathtaking. I understood why people find strength and the majesty of God in the awe-inspiring peaks. The geography of the holy land is somewhat different. The Church of the Transfiguration stands on Mount Tabor at only 1,886 metres. The views across Israel are still amazing, though. I am truly grateful for the privilege, and for the generosity of others that meant I could visit both places.

We read today of the disciples, who had perhaps been hoping for a rest, overcome by fear at what they saw and heard atop a high mountain. They could see Moses and Elijah – representing the law and the prophets. God's voice was heard. They truly were in the presence of the divine.

Is what Peter says unhelpful? It is often cited as an example of his tendency to blurt out something daft (although that tendency is exactly why I love Peter – there is hope for us all!). I think it's possible that he wanted to show his love for Jesus, to keep him safe in this holy place and away from the increasing danger in Jerusalem.

Peter, James and John could see the glory of God in the dazzling garments. The change to Jesus' garments calls to mind the story of the woman with a haemorrhage who was healed just by touching the hem of his cloak. It makes me consider just how Jesus' power and glory can be revealed. Was it any easier for these disciples, who'd had a glimpse of a different reality, to understand who Jesus was? They were seeing the impossible made possible with God.

For the Lord is a great God, and a great King above all gods. In his hand are the depths of the earth; the heights of the mountains are his also. (Psalm 95:3–4)

SARA BATTS

WEDNESDAY 18 MARCH   **ACTS 7:1–2, 54–60**

Heavenly glory

But filled with the Holy Spirit, [Stephen] gazed into heaven and saw the glory of God and Jesus standing at the right hand of God. (NRSV)

According to recent figures, over 200 million Christians in 50 countries face severe persecution for their faith. Stephen is the first martyr of the church. Chosen as one of the first deacons (6:1–6), he was 'full of grace and power' (6:8). Falsely accused of blasphemy, Stephen gives a stirring speech outlining the history of rejection of prophets. Others try to argue with him, but 'could not withstand the wisdom and the Spirit with which he spoke' (6:10).

Despite – because of – this great wisdom, Stephen's speech enrages his listeners. Just before they drag him outside to be stoned, he sees a vision of the glory of God and Jesus: the Son of Man standing at God's right hand, reminding us of Daniel 7.

This vision at a time of anger and violence reassures Stephen. Praying forgiveness for his persecutors is a clear echo of Jesus' words on the cross (Luke 23:34). Stephen is imitating Christ. He follows Jesus' lead in forgiving those who have caused his death.

Stephen's death is peaceful – the Greek says that he 'fell asleep'. That sits in contrast to his violent stoning. I think this helps emphasise the idea that death is not the end – he had seen the glory of Jesus at God's right hand and was not afraid.

Those who were listening to Stephen 'covered their ears'. They did not want to hear what he could see. They did not want to join in with his vision. The vision of glory was for Stephen, and for him alone. Sometimes we might long for others to share our vision, to see what we see of Jesus – to know him as we know him – yet they cover their ears. All we can do is pray, and leave it to God.

Loving God, we thank you for Stephen. We pray for all those who have died because of their faith. We pray for those Christians in our world today who risk death and imprisonment because of their faith in you.

SARA BATTS

THURSDAY 19 MARCH ACTS 8:26–40

Heaven-sent help

Then Philip began to speak, and starting with this scripture, he proclaimed to him the good news about Jesus. (NRSV)

Have you ever greeted a welcome visitor as an angel? 'Heaven must have sent you,' we say, as the right person arrives at the right time to solve a problem or relieve us of a burden. When we feel out of our depth, a wise and sensitive guide can help us to regain confidence and balance. That is, if we are brave enough to ask for assistance in the first place. I don't think I am the only person who has ever wanted to save face and not admit I didn't understand something – I am known as one who will ask the awkward question!

For the troubled Ethiopian, Philip really was 'heaven sent'. Guided by an angel of the Lord, Philip approaches a chariot on a wilderness road in order to hear the Ethiopian reading – but not understanding – Isaiah. Philip appears just when he is needed, and beginning with the passage from Isaiah, explains the good news about Jesus. The Ethiopian (oh, I wish we knew his name!) is baptised by the side of the road – at which point the Spirit of the Lord snatches Philip away. That must have been a truly strange, but life-changing, experience for the unnamed Ethiopian.

We might not always understand what we read, even with notes to help us explore ideas about a Bible passage. There are many ways to approach scripture. For example, imagining ourselves in the scene can be a powerful way to connect ideas and meaning. Reading very slowly and carefully might give us a word or phrase to investigate or pray.

God might not always send us a Philip, but he will always help us find new understanding of his word. And we might be a Philip to other people.

Give God thanks for the people who have helped you know his word. Ask him to show you how you might be a blessing to others who struggle to come to understand.

SARA BATTS

FRIDAY 20 MARCH ACTS 9:1–19

Who is Jesus?

Now as he was going along and approaching Damascus, suddenly a light from heaven flashed around him. He fell to the ground and heard a voice saying to him, 'Saul, Saul, why do you persecute me?' (NRSV)

Did you have a 'Damascus Road' experience of suddenly coming to faith? Or were you like me? I was gradually curious about what others saw in Jesus and tentatively allowed myself to be drawn in – but at the same time, I questioned everything, unsure if I wanted to make a commitment.

Jesus first asks Saul a question: 'Why do you persecute me?' Throughout the gospels, Jesus asks questions of those who follow and listen to him. His questioning appeals both to our reason and our emotions and allows time for a response.

A God who could create a universe could presumably choose to overrule the will of one man, creating for himself the perfect evangelist and pastor. But he doesn't – he chooses Saul… like he chose Moses, Mary, Isaiah, Philip and the others we have encountered. There are many days I wish I had been instantly made perfect at ordination (a heads-up – this doesn't happen to any clergy person!) but God works with me in the midst of my flaws. He wants our reaction to him to come from our own free will and our own longing for him.

Saul asks, 'Who are you?' and that is the question that many will ask as they come to meet Jesus. We have witnesses in the Bible, throughout the history of the church and among our contemporaries who can help us answer the question – not just with our head, as we read the stories told about Jesus' ministry during his life, but also with our heart as we hear the stories of those who witness to his love and power from the resurrection onwards.

What is your answer to the question, 'Who is Jesus?' Where might our answers to the questions take us if we wholeheartedly respond – and are willing to be led?

SARA BATTS

SATURDAY 21 MARCH   **ACTS 10:1–34**

Go and tell!

While Peter was still thinking about the vision, the Spirit said to him, 'Look, three men are searching for you. Now get up, go down, and go with them without hesitation; for I have sent them.' (NRSV)

We have followed the history of our faith through prophets' visions, appearances of angels and God's own revelation of himself. We finish with a passage showing how the message of peace in Jesus Christ began to spread across the world.

Have you ever been about to message someone, and they've called you? It's a nice coincidence – but here the Spirit is definitely working to bring Cornelius and Peter together. Their intertwined visions make for exciting reading.

Cornelius is a devout man. He responds in two ways to the vision of the angel of God. Firstly, he's terrified – a perfectly normal reaction. We've seen others feel the same in the past few days! Secondly, he does what he's asked. He summons two slaves and a soldier and sends them off to Joppa.

Peter, meanwhile, is being greatly puzzled at a vision of a sheet full of animals and a command not to call profane what God has called clean. As he's pondering on what this might mean, Cornelius' men arrive.

I can imagine how this story would play out if it were directed for a film. We'd have shots showing Cornelius' devotion and Peter's firm grasp of food laws. Then we'd see the terrifying angel – cut to Peter's trance – cut to Cornelius – back and forth until the two men finally meet.

Our attempts to share the gospel might not be quite so neatly choreographed. We have messy conversations and frustrating misunderstandings. We might not feel quite so eloquent as post-Pentecost Peter is. We might long for others to have sudden insight on their Damascus Road. And yet… ours might just be the kind action, friendly word or caring example that opens up the gospel for another, continuing the work that Peter began so many years ago.

'All the prophets testify about him that everyone who believes in him receives forgiveness of sins through his name' (Acts 10:43).

SARA BATTS

From the beginning: Genesis 1—11

Tracy Williamson writes:

Welcome to this journey together through Genesis 1—11. It is a fascinating and challenging story that has made me laugh, cry and pray with a new longing to live my life wholeheartedly for God and be ready to obey his call.

I love reminiscing with friends, looking back on special times in our lives, and sharing laughter, tears and poignant memories. As I explored these chapters looking back to the beginning of time, I felt that same joy bubbling in my heart. Like repeated refrains in a song, the truth that kept confronting me was that from the very beginning God had an amazing plan both for this universe and for humankind and that plan is still unfolding today.

Travel through these chapters with me and discover the wonder of God's vision and the depths of his grace. Be encouraged and healed by the knowledge that you were made in his image and matter more to him than words can say. Know that when catastrophe hits or when you mess up and let him down, he is still with you and will never give up on you. Be challenged as you consider how he called individuals to a certain path and what happened as they obeyed or disobeyed. Realise in a new way that God knows and feels the breadth of our emotions – after all, our ability to rejoice and feel pain, anger and love all come from him. Meet with him just as Adam did and know he delights in your friendship and loves to speak with you. Walk with him as Noah did and be ready to hear him call you into action.

I pray that you will be blessed as I was blessed and that these reflections will help you draw closer to your God.

SUNDAY 22 MARCH   **GENESIS 1:1–25**

God's vision

In the beginning, God created the heavens and the earth. Now the earth was formless and empty, darkness was over the surface of the deep and the Spirit of God was hovering over the waters. And God said, 'Let there be light' and there was light. (NIV)

Do you know that God loves to transform every area of darkness in our lives? This passage teaches us that while God is almighty, he has always loved us and had beautiful plans for us.

Here we see the birthing of God's awesome vision for this world and how right from the beginning he planned a universe that would be a pointer to heaven's glory. He planned for there to be beauty, light and life and for humankind to live in an incredible partnership with him. He created time and stepped into it, seeing the nothingness yet knowing exactly how he would transform it. Everything he made was good and there was a sense of joyful adventure as he formed each part.

When reading this, I realised that the writer must have received revelation about God's extravagant joy in creating us. I thought, do I really know him like that? God longs for us to understand what he is like, that he delights to create beauty out of chaos. His plans are full of the details of love and that love is as real for us now as it was then.

Verse 2 says, 'The Spirit of God was hovering over the waters.' This same Spirit hovers over the dark areas in our thoughts and emotions, ready to transform them. Don't despair; God is speaking his plans over you and the Spirit will bring them to fruition. Don't be afraid. God is as full of delight today when creating beauty as he was at the beginning. Every detail is known and accounted for in his plans for you. He speaks love and light and new life is born. Let's be encouraged, for this history of creation is the ongoing reality of his loving, creative work in each of our lives today.

Spend some time rereading this passage from Genesis 1. Are you aware of barren areas in your life? Ask God to speak his words of beauty and creative life into them. Drink in his love and joy in you.

TRACY WILLIAMSON

MONDAY 23 MARCH **GENESIS 1:26—2:7**

Made in his image

God said 'Let us make mankind in our image, in our likeness, so that they may rule over… all the creatures…' So God created mankind in his own image, in the image of God he created them; male and female he created them. (NIV)

How incredible that we were made in his image! The opening verses of Genesis show how much God delighted in creating the universe, but he only chose to develop a loving communicative relationship with humankind.

It is wonderful how the Father, Son and Holy Spirit planned how we would carry attributes of the divine in our very DNA, that we would be in partnership with him, even trusting us to rule the beautiful world he had just made. Just as parents long to see something of themselves in their children, so God longed that something of his character and glory would be revealed through each one of us.

Let's make a determined choice to start to live in this truth, as it's vital for our spiritual growth. It's so easy to think negatively about ourselves. I believed for years that I was stupid. It's hard to refute words that are coming at you constantly and, as my stepfather shouted at me, I took his words in and allowed them to become my identity. Even after becoming a Christian, my self-talk was constantly full of negatives.

Many of us undermine ourselves, but this passage in Genesis shows God's true view of us and this should be our yardstick. Once when I was praying about my deep feelings of shame, God brought these life-changing words to my mind: 'Could I have created my child with less joy, to be less beautiful than a flower, a bird or a tree? As beautiful as they are and as much as they reveal my splendour, they cannot talk with me. I have made you to be joined in love and be part of me, and through all that you are and do to thus reveal my beauty.'

You too have been created to reveal his beauty.

Thank you, Father, that you made me in your image. Please forgive me for all the negative ways I have thought and spoken about myself. Please help me learn to live in the truth of your love for me.

TRACY WILLIAMSON

TUESDAY 24 MARCH **GENESIS 2:8–23**

A beautiful friendship

Now the Lord God had formed out of the ground all the wild animals and all the birds in the sky. He brought them to the man to see what he would name them; and whatever the man called each living creature, that was its name. (NIV)

Do you have a special friend that you love to spend time with? That love of companionship is something we see throughout all creation – at my home, for example, my hearing dog Goldie loves to snuggle up and play with his doggy companion, guide dog Saffie. It's clear they really enjoy each other's company.

That quality of joy in companionship comes from God, who in these early chapters of Genesis reveals his delight in being with Adam. Genesis 3:8 describes the Lord as walking in the garden in the cool of the day and this appears to have been the time he regularly came to meet up with Adam and Eve. We can only imagine the wonder of their times together in this period before the fall. But the good news is that through Jesus, we are restored back to real companionship with God, able to know him and hear his voice.

One thing that really inspires me is the deep respect God showed Adam in asking him to partner with him by naming all the animals he had just created. Adam must have been full of wonder as he encountered the stunning butterfly followed by the stomping weight of the elephant, followed by… Every name that burst from his lips became The Name.

God also understood Adam's need of a human companion. Friends can be more aware than family of their loved ones' needs, and act to help them. It was in that spirit that God created Eve for Adam, saying 'It is not good for the man to be alone.'

I have experienced God encouraging me or comforting me when I've been sad, and I've also experienced him working with me to bless others. I long to go deeper in my friendship and partnership with him. Do you long for this too?

God has chosen you and me to be his friends. He enables us to hear him and trusts us to do his wonderful works through the Holy Spirit's enabling. What does he want to do together with you today?

TRACY WILLIAMSON

WEDNESDAY 25 MARCH **GENESIS 2:25—3:7**

Whose voice?

When the woman saw that the fruit of the tree was good for food and pleasing to the eye, and also desirable for gaining wisdom, she took some and ate it. She also gave some to her husband, who was with her, and he ate it. Then the eyes of both of them were opened, and they realised they were naked. (NIV)

Whose voice are we listening to?

There is a key phrase in this account of the fall: 'When the woman saw…' Seeing is a wonderful gift but there is a different kind of seeing, an inner seeing, fuelled by who we listen to or agree with in our hearts. It may be a sudden understanding enabling us to take life-changing steps, but if it comes from the wrong source it can lead us to 'see' things that cripple our faith.

Like Eve, we have an enemy who loves to feed us with twisted interpretations of the truth. He is very devious and works to sow doubts about God, ourselves and others. He twisted Eve's responses, implying that God was lying and a spoilsport for trying to keep them from having divine knowledge. It's at that point that the telling phrase, 'when the woman saw', is written. It is as if the devil's insinuations gave her 'revelation' that superseded all she'd already experienced of God's goodness and love. As she listened, the truth of God's character faded from her consciousness.

Has this been happening with you too? In my life, I find it's devil-fuelled insecurity and over-anxiety that most rob me. It's so important that we keep focusing on God and listening to his voice even above the significant people in our lives.

Adam chose to go along with Eve and ate the fruit she gave him, despite God having spoken to him directly. The tragedy of the fall is not that they ate the forbidden fruit so much as they listened to the wrong voice and 'saw' in the wrong way. The resulting sin and shame have affected us ever since, but in his great love God restores us; his call, to love him above all, is unchanging.

'A bright cloud covered them, and a voice from the cloud said, "This is my Son, whom I love; with him I am well pleased. Listen to him!"' (Matthew 17:5, NIV). Lord, please help me to listen well.

TRACY WILLIAMSON

THURSDAY 26 MARCH GENESIS 3:8–24

Fear, blame and God's faithfulness

But the Lord God called to the man, 'Where are you?' He answered, 'I heard you in the garden, and I was afraid because I was naked; so I hid.' (NIV)

Our actions have repercussions. One of the most destructive effects of Adam and Eve's disobedience was fear. Before, they'd had no idea what fear was, now, they were too afraid to face God, with whom they'd enjoyed unparalleled friendship. Fear immediately controlled their reactions, causing deep shame. It has been a catastrophic part of human life ever since, birthing reactions like control, anger, cruelty, mockery and murder.

Fear makes us hide ourselves and the truth of who we are. Instead of joyful confidence, we distrust everything and lash out at others in order to protect ourselves. God wanted them to take responsibility for their own sin so he could forgive them. But they refused and blame became the new order, with Adam even attributing responsibility to God. Eve, too, blamed the serpent rather than just confessing what she'd done. We all fall into this trap; I share a home with my great friend Marilyn, but we can so easily become defensive and start blaming each other for the slightest things.

But the wonderful thing to focus on is that God came and searched for Adam and Eve, calling them out of their hiding places, and he does the same for us. He had to judge them, but he still loved them, still spoke to them, still guided and provided for them and still set in place his plan for redemption.

He loves you and me with that same powerfully healing love, too.

Fear has been a huge part of my life and even today I still battle with its effects. But I am winning that battle because of God's faithful, ongoing love. I am becoming the joyful, confident woman he created me to be.

Let's stop giving the devil room and allow God to lead us into wholeness.

Father, thank you for your persevering love. Forgive me for following Adam and Eve's path and opening myself up to patterns of fear and blame. I choose to receive your wonderful healing and peace.

TRACY WILLIAMSON

FRIDAY 27 MARCH **GENESIS 4**

The growing of a man

The Lord said to Cain, 'Why are you angry? Why is your face downcast? If you do what is right, will you not be accepted? But if you do not do what is right, sin is crouching at your door; it desires to have you, but you must rule over it.' (NIV)

Have you ever thought: how can things just carry on when my own world has come to an end?

Genesis 4 shows that life does indeed carry on, even after the most catastrophic events, but we always have a choice. Will we become swamped by the memories or will we trust that God is calling us to grow even in the area of our deepest pain?

Verse 1 is significant: '[Eve] became pregnant and gave birth to Cain. She said, "With the help of the Lord I have brought forth a man."' Although Cain would murder his own brother, God would not abandon him, working towards making him into a better man.

God never gives up on us but he cannot force us into our true destiny; the choice is always ours. He said to Cain, 'Sin is crouching at your door; it desires to have you, but you must rule over it.' If Cain had listened to God, that terrible outcome of his jealousy may have been averted.

What do we do with our dark thoughts and feelings? Life was so tough for that first family after the joy of Eden. And life can be so tough for us, too. How do we respond when others receive favour but never us? When things go wrong whatever we try? It's so easy for those dark thoughts to fill our hearts, but the more we harbour them the more power they have to control us.

Maybe you feel, like Cain, that God can never forgive you. But God still loved Cain and guided him. Cain ultimately founded a city. God loves you too and will empower you to fulfil your true calling in him.

Lord, thank you for this understanding of the importance of dealing with my dark and painful feelings. Forgive me for allowing them to control my choices. Please change me and lead me into my full, God-given destiny.

TRACY WILLIAMSON

SATURDAY 28 MARCH   **GENESIS 5**

Our lives count

When Adam had lived 130 years he had a son in his own likeness, in his own image; and he named him Seth. After Seth was born, Adam lived 800 years and had other sons and daughters. Altogether, Adam lived a total of 930 years, and then he died. (NIV)

Do you know how significant you are?

I don't know about you, but I find genealogy chapters in the Bible rather boring! I tend to skip through them looking for more interesting stories. Yet today, God spoke through this chapter with the thought: 'Your life counts.'

Your life counts. You are significant in God's eyes. This is the heart of this chapter's message. In these post-fall generations, God was developing the human race and seeking those who would once again reflect his image. We know little about their lives other than that they lived many years and had children! But in God's eyes, they were significant enough to name in his holy records. It's important you know that you too have your place in his holy records. You are significant.

But God defines significance very differently. He's not looking for great feats or promotions so much as how we choose to live and love in all the little details of our lives.

Seth was born when Adam was 130. After the devastation of effectively losing both sons through Cain's actions, Adam now had the joy of a son 'in his own likeness, in his own image'.

These words are inspiring because they mirror what God planned for Adam and humankind. We are all made in God's image, as the start of this chapter reminds us, but we are also meant to be passing on his attributes. I believe that in that long gap before Seth was born, Adam was learning to let God be in the centre again, to give God his regrets and to listen again, allowing his actions to be prompted by God's love rather than the old bitterness. Thus Seth was born, reflecting the true Adam and in turn passing those attributes to his own children.

Thank you, Lord, that I matter to you and my life counts. Please help me to live with you at the centre and to reveal, and pass on to others, the beauty of your character.

TRACY WILLIAMSON

SUNDAY 29 MARCH   **GENESIS 6**

God's grief and the power of a holy life

God saw that human evil was out of control… [He] was sorry that he had made the human race in the first place; it broke his heart… But Noah was different; God liked what he saw in Noah. (MSG)

In my ministry, I meet many people who are heartbroken through the devastating actions of their loved ones. I too have known the pain of trusting in someone, only to have them abuse me. In this chapter, we are given a glimpse into God's pain. Unlike us, God alone sees the whole truth and he saw that 'every inclination of… the human heart was only evil all the time' (v. 5, NIV). From my own experience of broken trust, I can only imagine God's deep sorrow. He who had created us to reveal his beauty was now filled with pain and grieved that he had made us. How heartbreaking, not just for God but for humankind too. I sense that someone reading this is also experiencing the agony of betrayal and grief. God understands like no one else can. He is with you in your pain and, just as he made a way for humankind to be redeemed, so he will bring restoration to you.

I find it sobering to realise that in the face of God's agonising decision to annihilate the whole of creation, it was just one man, Noah, who changed things. 'Noah found favour in the eyes of the Lord… [he] was a righteous man… and he walked faithfully with God' (vv. 8–9, NIV).

If you feel you don't have any influence, think of Noah. Because of his quiet love for God, the whole course of history was changed. We celebrate him for building the ark, but that came after. He found favour with God because he lived for him. His love for God made him shine like gold in the midst of the darkness and enabled God to amend his plan. The resulting judgement was still catastrophic, but was undergirded with mercy and the promise of a new beginning; all because of one man.

Ponder further this glimpse into God also experiencing heartbreak and grief. Offer him all the sadness in your own heart and ask him to fill you with his love so that, like Noah, you can be a holy influencer.

TRACY WILLIAMSON

MONDAY 30 MARCH   **GENESIS 7**

Living through the flood

In the six hundredth year of Noah's life, on the seventeenth day of the second month – on that day all the springs of the great deep burst forth, and the floodgates of the heavens were opened. And rain fell on the earth forty days and forty nights. (NIV)

Noah's wife writes: I worried Noah was going mad as he worked with manic urgency. What was all this talk of God's judgement? One day, through deep sobs, he told me of his encounter and how we would all be destroyed unless we went inside the ark. I dismissed it, of course, but then animals started arriving – elephants, bears, lions… all heading straight towards Noah as if a hand was guiding them. I screamed but they just filed peacefully on to the ark. How was that possible? These were wild creatures! Day after day, more came. What was going on? Surely, we wouldn't really have to get in there too? Surely Noah had got it wrong?

It was terrible when the waters came. The sky turned black, the air shivered and the very ground started moaning, a chilling scary sound. Before our eyes, cracks appeared, spewing fountains of black water over our feet. People screamed, frantic to escape, hands clutching, faces gargoyles of terror. Where we'd all been reluctant to enter the ark, there was now a panic to get in and shut the door. The wind roared and torrential rain flung itself to earth, but suddenly a miraculous force slammed the door shut. We huddled together, terrified, as the ark twisted and groaned as it was struck repeatedly by large objects. I thought it would break apart, but incredibly it stayed upright. Endless days went by as we tried to shut our ears to the cacophony of screeches from the animals and the thunder of rain. But one day, when I felt overwhelmed with the noise, darkness and stench of fear, I heard God's voice, deep in my heart, clear, beautiful: 'Peace, I am with you.' My fury drained away. Noah was right. God was with us. With him, we would survive.

Thank you, Lord, that even in times of darkness and terror, when my world collapses and I am overwhelmed, you are with me. May my heart be open to your voice of peace today.

TRACY WILLIAMSON

TUESDAY 31 MARCH   **GENESIS 8**

Worship: the door to God's presence

Then Noah built an altar to the Lord and, taking some of all the clean animals and clean birds, he sacrificed burnt offerings on it. The Lord smelled the pleasing aroma and said in his heart: 'Never again will I curse the ground because of humans, even though every inclination of the human heart is evil.' (NIV)

Anyone who has witnessed the devastation of a bad accident or natural disaster will have a glimpse into what Noah and his family felt as they finally stepped from the ark back on to dry land. It must have been a horrific sight. I'm no scientist so I've no idea what state the corpses would have been in after nearly half a year underwater, but the evidence of death and devastation must have been phenomenal. Were they worried about the countless 'unknowns' before them?

Could they get down from Mount Ararat on legs weakened by the months of confinement? Could they see properly after being in the dark for so long? How could they start all over again?

In our own life journey, we can become overly anxious about unknowns. How will I cope if I'm left on my own? What if I become sick? What will we do if we have to move…?

A key from this story is that the very first thing Noah did after leaving the ark was to build an altar to the Lord for worship. Yes, they'd been through an overwhelmingly traumatic time and now faced more devastation. But they had come through. God had been with them. They were alive because of his mercy. I believe that act of worship protected them from ongoing trauma and enabled them to step into their new beginning.

Will we, like them, choose to make an offering to God of our love and heart-focus, whatever we are going through? Such worship opens the door to the power of his presence and life-giving promises. They could now face rebuilding their lives without the fear of this ever happening again. What promise does God want to give you today?

'God is our refuge and strength, an ever-present help in trouble. Therefore we will not fear, though the earth give way and the mountains fall into the heart of the sea, though its waters roar and foam' (Psalm 46:1–3).

TRACY WILLIAMSON

WEDNESDAY 1 APRIL **GENESIS 9:1–7**

Be fruitful

God blessed Noah and his sons, saying to them, 'Be fruitful and increase in number and fill the earth.' (NIV)

After the devastation of the flood came the blessing of a new purpose.

Do you know that God blesses us to live with purpose? We think of blessing as being happy and having good things happen, but it's also to do with stepping into your calling and living it out effectively. We all have a mandate from God, a divine purpose that he calls us to fulfil and, in these verses, we see God speaking directly to Noah and his family, giving them the mandate to be fruitful, increase in number and fill the earth. God had just wiped out most of humankind. Now he wants to see the world repopulated and Noah's family are the ones he has ordained to start that process.

Be fruitful – what did this mean? In the Bible, fruitfulness is associated with character as well as with growth. I believe he was giving them the blessing of being sons again, called to reveal his goodness, a privilege that had diminished after the fall.

God then speaks to them about their authority over creation: 'The fear and dread of you will fall on all the beasts of the earth, and on all the birds in the sky.' God was honouring their inner maturing throughout their months in the ark. Their stature had grown because they'd discovered what it meant to rely on God and trust in him for the future. They'd had to look after the animals and ensure none would die. As God continues teaching them how to choose to live wisely, he also builds their moral understanding, that their actions will always have 'an accounting'.

Like Noah's family, whatever our situations, God is calling us to mature into his beloved children, carrying his authority on this earth. Will we live in that calling?

Father God, I feel challenged and long to grow into my own calling to carry your authority and be your representative on this earth. Please teach me as you taught Noah, and empower me by your Holy Spirit.

TRACY WILLIAMSON

THURSDAY 2 APRIL   **GENESIS 9:8–29**

Covenant and curse

And God said, 'This is the sign of the covenant I am making between me and you and every living creature with you, a covenant for all generations to come: I have set my rainbow in the clouds, and it will be the sign of the covenant between me and the earth.' (NIV)

This passage opens with God's covenantal promise to humankind and every living creature that 'never again will all life be destroyed by the waters of a flood; never again will there be a flood to destroy the earth'.

Unlike other covenant passages, this was not about an agreement between two parties for both to fulfil. This was all on God's side. He was promising something that he, as God, would be 100% committed to fulfilling. He was choosing to limit his right to exert judgement on the earth by wiping life out. From now on, he would work solely in the hearts of humankind and would ultimately bring judgement on sin through the death of his own Son.

God chose the rainbow as the symbol of that promise and today it is one of the key symbols of Christian hope. When we see the beautiful arc of colour spanning the sky after a downpour of rain, it gives us courage to keep trusting and facing our difficult circumstances.

God told Noah that whenever the rainbow appeared in the sky, he would remember his covenant promise. God wanted to instil awareness that he is constantly thinking of us, constantly living by the covenant he has made, that he is working on our behalf and is not against us.

Life continues in all its ramifications, as is shown when this significant moment is followed by the tragedy of Noah's shame and the subsequent curse over his youngest son Ham and his descendants. It brings home to me the often-unrealised impact of our words and actions – that they can have such tremendous effect for good or bad. I long to be like Shem, not Ham, choosing to react in wise and godly ways to life's situations. What about you?

Lord God, thank you for giving us the rainbow of your covenant promise. Help me to live in its truth and in all my words and reactions become more and more an ambassador of your love and goodness.

TRACY WILLIAMSON

FRIDAY 3 APRIL   **GENESIS 10**

The forming of nations

These are the clans of Noah's sons, according to their lines of descent, within their nations. From these the nations spread out over the earth after the flood. (NIV)

On Wednesday, we saw how God gave Noah the mandate to 'increase in number and fill the earth'. Now in Genesis 10, we see how that began to be fulfilled as Noah's descendants spread over the earth, forming unique people groups. Most of the chapter is filled with their names, their tribes and the territories they established. We read this now knowing, what will soon be unfolding: the history of Abram and the forming of Israel. At that time, though, they were just living their daily lives, growing up, developing as individuals, forging a living, marrying and having children. In effect, they were living as we live, but in a very different culture.

The thing that strikes me is that behind the scenes, God was at work and it is clear that every person mattered to God. They were born at the right time and unknowingly were playing their part in the evolving of history. For example, it says in verses 8–12 that Nimrod the son of Cush was a mighty warrior before the Lord. Through using his God-given strength, he founded powerful cities like Nineveh and Babylon.

Many of the tribes, such as the Canaanites and Philistines, went on to become bitter enemies of the Israelites, yet they still mattered enough to God that they were named in his holy records. They were part of his evolving plans for the whole world and thus of redemption. Everyone matters to him, including those who are hostile to his love.

God is constantly seeking out those who, like Noah and Nimrod, choose to live for him. He may call us to do things that change history or to simply let his love direct our daily choices. Whatever his call, our faithful obedience will bring significant effects for his kingdom.

Be encouraged – God is at work in you and those you love. We may not all have children but we do all leave a legacy that will leave its mark on those who follow. What will your legacy be?

TRACY WILLIAMSON

SATURDAY 4 APRIL   **GENESIS 11**

Our pride or God's call?

They said, 'Come, let us build ourselves a city, with a tower that reaches to the heavens, so that we may make a name for ourselves; otherwise we will be scattered over the face of the whole earth.' But the Lord came down to see the city and the tower the people were building. (NIV)

We end this series with some challenging thoughts from the story of the Tower of Babel. Commentators suggest that Babel may have actually happened soon after the flood rather than at the time suggested by its position in Genesis, and that Babel was the cause of Noah's descendants scattering so quickly and developing new languages. This indicates that although God had given them the mandate to fill the earth, their focus was on their own plans.

It's very easy to assent to God's commands but apply them in a way that makes us feel comfortable. God told them to 'fill the earth', but at the start of Genesis 11 we read that 'they found a plain in Shinar and settled there'. Their interpretation of God's command was to huddle together, not spread out, but God wanted the whole earth to be filled.

Amazingly, we see this again at the end of the chapter: Terah the father of Abram 'set out from Ur of the Chaldeans to go to Canaan. But when they came to Haran, they settled there.' It's clear from God's subsequent call to Abram (12:1) that he had ordained Terah's original journey to Canaan, so why did they settle in Haran? And why did those earlier families settle in Shinar rather than obeying God's command to spread throughout the earth?

The answer was rebellion. They wanted a city so they didn't have to obey God's call, and they wanted a tower so that they could become famous. God wanted their security to be in him and for them to know the joy of his affirmation. But because of pride, they followed their own desires.

As the curtain closes on the first act of history, the challenge remains: Will we dare to listen and respond wholeheartedly to God's call?

Loving Father, thank you with all my heart, that you never give up on us.
TRACY WILLIAMSON

Want to know more about Genesis 1—11?

This *Really Useful Guide* to Genesis 1—11 opens up afresh what can be a familiar text. In showing us how to engage with these stories, Rebecca Watson gives us background information about how, why and when Genesis was written, tips for reading and studying, and a summary of how Genesis 1—11 fits into the biblical story. Written in bite-sized chunks and full of jargon-free practical guidance, this book will give you more confidence to engage with the Bible and a greater understanding of the nature of God.

Really Useful Guides: Genesis 1—11
Rebecca Watson
978 0 85746 791 1 £5.99
brfonline.org.uk

Holy ground

Rosemary Green writes:

'We'd like to commission you to write 14 notes taking the readers through Mark's gospel account of Holy Week and Easter.' When I first read the editor's invitation, I thought; 'What a privilege to write about the most momentous week of Jesus' time on earth.' They are chapters that are largely familiar to most of us, yet there are always new depths to be explored and we can never spend too much time meditating on Jesus' death and resurrection. It is a chance to think afresh for myself, and then to help the readers, to meditate on those events.

Then I had a problem. It would make sense, as we walk through Holy Week 2020, to try to write for the day of the week that matches the gospel events. But our celebration of Easter Day comes halfway through my allotted days. So the first week of these notes matches the daily events in Jerusalem as near as I could, while after Easter we look back at some of Jesus' teaching in the days preceding the crucifixion.

The next question was how to help us to see those events with fresh eyes. That was when I decided to write each day as it might have been experienced by someone who was there. I admit that this approach uses a measure of imagination. But it also means looking carefully at the Bible verses in front of us, as well as using insights from other parts of scripture.

I hope it will always be clear what is fact and what is imagined in the reflections and emotions. I hope, too, that it will bring scripture alive in a new way, and bring home some aspects of the events that we might otherwise ignore. They were real people who were present. While most of my 'writers' were Jesus' followers, I have included some who were not.

Mark's gospel is thought by most to be the first of the gospels to be written, perhaps in AD66–70 – possibly by Mark, but possibly an unknown Christian.

SUNDAY 5 APRIL   **MARK 11:1–11**

A regal ride

When they brought the colt to Jesus and threw their cloaks over it, he sat on it. Many people spread their cloaks on the road, while others spread branches they had cut in the fields. Those who went ahead and those who followed shouted, 'Hosanna!' (NIV)

A pilgrim from Galilee writes in his diary: I've made the Passover pilgrimage from my home in Capernaum to Jerusalem each year since I was twelve. Every part of it is a rich experience. One of the highlights of the journey always comes when we reach the end of the 25-mile ascent, as the track rises over 800 metres through the desert from the Jordan valley. Soon after we reach the villages of Bethphage and Bethany, we top the brow of the hill. Suddenly, the panorama of Jerusalem is in front of us.

I like to arrive when the late afternoon sun is shining across the Kedron valley on to the gilded temple in front of us. It's always special – but today was something else! The Rabbi Jesus and his friends were ahead of us. When we caught up with them, he was riding on a donkey foal that he had borrowed from one of the villagers. I don't know who started all the excitement. We joined in with the crowd who were shouting acclamations from Psalm 118, which I'm told was written to celebrate the triumph of Judas Maccabeus when he overthrew the temple-violating Antiochus Epiphanes 2,000 years ago. We made a path for Jesus with our cloaks and with branches. It reminded me of Zechariah writing of the Messiah king coming to Jerusalem 'riding on a colt, the foal of a donkey'. We followed him right down to the temple; there he just stopped, looked carefully round, and then left, as it was twilight.

I have been impressed when I have heard Jesus teaching in Galilee, and I have seen some of his miracles. But is he really a king? Our religious leaders will not like that; neither will our hated Roman overlords.

As Jesus approaches the climax of his life, we see him even more unafraid of publicity and confrontation. Think: How do I cope in a climate hostile to Christianity?

ROSEMARY GREEN

MONDAY 6 APRIL MARK 11:12–20

Confrontation

When they arrived back in Jerusalem, Jesus entered the Temple and began to drive out the people buying and selling animals for sacrifices. He knocked over the tables of the money changers and the chairs of those selling doves, and he stopped everyone from using the Temple as a marketplace. (NLT)

Two priests talk together.

Priest 1: Who does this fellow Jesus think he is? Yesterday he rode into Jerusalem on a donkey, escorted by a cheering rabble. Today he had the nerve to charge into the temple area and overthrow the merchants' tables. He's upsetting our whole sacrificial system!

Priest 2: He's crazy, but he's dangerous, too. He's threatening our authority. Look at the crowd that clustered round him. Jerusalem is volatile enough anyway this week before Passover, with a million visitors in the city. We don't want to upset the Roman authorities, especially when Pontius Pilate has left his seaside palace in Caesarea to come here as well.

Priest 1: He's clever as well – crafty, anyway. I've heard he has a cunning way of manipulating questions when the Pharisees or Sadducees try to show how wrong he is. He manages to turn it round and put them in a difficult position. And he seems to know the scriptures better than most of us do. Did you notice how he quoted Isaiah, 'a house of prayer for all nations'?

Priest 2: He has some magic power, too. I've heard talk of many miraculous cures from chronic illness and disability, and even demon possession.

Priest 1: Do you know that old fig tree near Bethany? A friend told me that he cursed it because it had no early season green figs, to show promise of the main crop. My friend thought he was giving a message of judgement against Israel.

Priest 2: We need to get rid of him! But what if he is more than just a crazy Messianic pretender?

Jesus' cursing of the unproductive fig-tree was an acted parable of judgement on people whose obedience to God was nominal. Is my obedience to Jesus nominal or true? Do I have a right fear of his judgement?

ROSEMARY GREEN

TUESDAY 7 APRIL 　　　　　　　　　　　　　　　　　　**MARK 12:1–12**

Too near the bone

Jesus then began to speak to them in parables: 'A man planted a vineyard…' Then the chief priests, the teachers of the law and the elders looked for a way to arrest him because they knew he had spoken the parable against them. But they were afraid of the crowd. (NIV)

A Pharisee reflects: This self-appointed rabbi Jesus is really getting under my skin! A country yokel from Galilee, with an ill-assorted rabble of followers – fishermen and the like – coming to teach publicly in the temple courts. The crowds seem to hang on his every word.

Today he told a story about a vineyard and the way the tenant farmers treated the owner's emissaries. It made me think of Isaiah 5 and his 'song of the vineyard', with its similar picture of a carefully tended vineyard, with its watchtower and its winepress. That vineyard yielded only bad grapes and had to be destroyed. Isaiah said, 'The vineyard of the Lord Almighty is the house of Israel.'

I am aware that we are the guardians of Israel's spiritual heritage. Is this Jesus trying to liken us to the tenants? The servants the owner sent: are they the prophets whom many of our forebears disregarded? And who does he mean by the son whom they killed?

I have heard that Jesus even claims to be able to forgive sin, but no one but God can do that. Does he think he is equal to God? That's blasphemy! I don't understand it all, but I am sure he is getting at us – Pharisees, teachers and priests alike.

We'll have to put our heads together and think of a way to get rid of this dangerous imposter, once and for all. It will have to be a good scheme to trap this cunning man and hoodwink the public. It must satisfy the Romans, too, if we want the death penalty.

This was another step in the Pharisees' escalating hostility. But even as I condemn them, I must never forget my own share in putting Jesus on the cross. Lord Jesus, thank you again that you died for my forgiveness.

ROSEMARY GREEN

WEDNESDAY 8 APRIL MARK 14:1–11

Generous devotion

A woman came with an alabaster jar of very expensive perfume… She broke the jar and poured the perfume on [Jesus'] head. Some of those present were saying indignantly to one another, 'Why this waste?…' [Jesus said] 'She has done a beautiful thing to me.' (NIV)

The woman reflects: Jesus, my Master. He's wonderful! I could never have imagined anyone like him. The men, his friends, round him; they admired him and wanted to please him. But they were so clumsy and often got it all wrong. How could I show how much I loved him? Specially just then. There was all the usual excitement around, with so many people coming to Jerusalem for Passover, but also a strange atmosphere of hate and suspicion. I sensed the religious authorities were getting even more hostile towards him.

How could I express my adoration for him? Then I remembered my alabaster jar of spikenard. I have treasured that for years, waiting for a special occasion to start using it, sparingly. I thought, that's how I can demonstrate what he's worth! Use all of it, unstintingly, for him. So while the men were reclining by the low table, waiting for the meal to be served, I crept up and poured the perfume freely over his head. The aroma was sweet, but there was astonishment all round, and outright indignation from Judas. Trust him to complain in his scornful, sanctimonious way, 'What a waste! That's worth a year's wages for a labourer! It could have been sold and the proceeds given to the poor fund.' I'd never liked that man, nor trusted him. I reckon some of it would have gone in his own pocket. Why did Jesus trust him with the common purse?

But my wonderful Master understood. His comments amazed and humbled me, when he said that my action would be remembered all round the world. But it was scary, too. 'She anointed my body for burial.' It was as if he was expecting to die soon.

Reflect honestly about where you stand on the spectrum from the woman's extravagant love to Judas' rejection of love. Pray about what God needs to change in you.

ROSEMARY GREEN

THURSDAY 9 APRIL   **MARK 14:43–53**

We ran away

The betrayer had arranged a signal with them: 'The one I kiss is the man; arrest him and lead him away under guard.' Going at once to Jesus, Judas said, 'Rabbi!' and kissed him. (NIV)

John Mark writes in his diary: What a full and emotional evening it has been! I've been hanging around on the edge, to watch. Two of Jesus' disciples came to our house today to prepare for their group to eat the Passover meal together; they were obviously expected. I don't know what went on in there, but I did see Judas sneaking out before the rest. Then they all trooped out to the Mount of Olives. Eight of them sat and waited, while Jesus first went on with his special trio, then further by himself. Peter, James and John dozed. I could just see Jesus in the distance, obviously praying intensely; it looked as if he was in deep pain. But when they all came back, his face exuded peace.

Suddenly the quiet was shattered by a noisy mob. Peter tried to defend Jesus and cut off a man's ear with his sword. But Jesus reprimanded him, touched the man's ear and it was healed. Amazing! Then Judas came up to Jesus, quietly, and kissed him. It felt a mockery; I think he was identifying Jesus to the ruffians, who seized him and dragged him off.

It was turmoil; we were all scared. Jesus' friends scattered in the dark. I wanted to stay and watch, but one of the mob tried to seize me. He grabbed my tunic, so I just let him have it, and ran away in my birthday suit. I'm ashamed that I didn't do more to defend Jesus. I feel as if I have let him down.

[*Rosemary*: I hope I have not made 2+2=5! Many people think that the young man in verse 53 is John Mark, whose mother regularly hosted the early Christians (Acts 12:13). So the upper room of Jesus' Passover may well have been in her house.]

We may deplore the disciples' desertion. But we live in a culture that increasingly disparages Christians. Do I stick up for Jesus? Or do I wimp out?
ROSEMARY GREEN

FRIDAY 10 APRIL MARK 15:11–32

Crucifixion

They brought Jesus to the place called Golgotha... Then they offered him wine mixed with myrrh, but he did not take it. And they crucified him. Dividing up his clothes, they cast lots to see what each would get. It was nine in the morning when they crucified him. (NIV)

A soldier writes to his wife: I never like taking part in a crucifixion. It's an inhumane way to treat even the worst criminal. There were three of them today; two were the usual ruffians, but the other was different. He seemed a real gentleman. The governor thought so too; he even referred to him as 'King of the Jews', and suggested his release. But the crowd only bayed louder for his death. Pilate caved in – he's a weak man.

First we flogged the prisoner; that's brutal enough, with the whips' many thongs and sharp stones. Then we had some fun with him – I'm ashamed of it now. We dressed him in regal purple, stuck a crown of three-inch long spiky thorns on his head. We paid him mock homage, hit his head, spat on him. Even in this humiliation, he took it with dignity. But he was too weak to carry the heavy crossbar, and we dragged out a bystander to do it. Despite his pain, he refused the pain-killing drugged wine we always offer before a crucifixion. Then we hammered the nails into his wrists and shins, and hoisted him up. We have to wait many hours, sometimes days, till a prisoner is dead. We whiled away time gambling for his clothes, while the passers-by, even the Jewish leaders, mocked him.

It was weird. At noon, the brightest part of the day, everything went dark – as black as midnight. It was eerily quiet. Then, after three hours a cry pierced the silence. This king cried out, 'My God, why have you forsaken me?' The sun shone again; we heard another cry. Then he died. I don't know who he was, but he has left a deep impression on me.

[*Rosemary*: The soldier's words bring home the physical brutality that Jesus endured. But surely even that pain was pale beside the agony of being separated from his heavenly Father as he bore the weight and ugliness of the garbage of the world's sin.]

He did it for you. He did it for me. Lord, thank you, thank you, thank you.

ROSEMARY GREEN

SATURDAY 11 APRIL   **MARK 15:33–47**

A secret disciple

Joseph of Arimathea, a prominent member of the Council… went boldly to Pilate and asked for Jesus' body… So Joseph bought some linen cloth, took down the body, wrapped it in the linen, and placed it in a tomb cut out of rock. (NIV)

Joseph of Arimathea writes in his diary: I have felt ashamed the last 48 hours. Ashamed of the way we, the Sanhedrin, treated Jesus. Even more ashamed of my own cowardice. At least I didn't vote for his death with the rest of the Council. But that opposition was ineffectual, and I'm ashamed that I have been fearful for so long. I have believed secretly in Jesus for many months, after Nicodemus told me of his night-time visit to Jesus and his puzzling conversation about rebirth. But for a long time I've kept quiet, afraid how the others might treat me, wondering how openness might affect my status or my wealth. Yet if Jesus really is the Messiah; if, as he says, 'he and his Father are one'; if he has come from God – then what I might lose is nothing compared with what he lost in coming to live on earth. And now he has lost his life.

    Yesterday was a gruesome day. Strange, too, with the hours of darkness in the middle of the day. Jesus bore his intense pain with huge dignity. That, and my shame, gave me the courage to go to Pilate when Jesus was dead and ask for his body to be taken down from the cross. Pilate was surprised he had died so quickly, and sent for the centurion in charge to check up. Then he released the body, and Nicodemus and I gave him a decent burial. I was glad I had already prepared a grave for myself and could give that to Jesus, glad to do the best we could for him. Nicodemus came out into the open as well, and brought some myrrh and aloes, but we had to work quickly so that it was finished before the sabbath started at dusk.

Lord, I often share Joseph's shame, when I behave like a secret disciple hiding my faith in Jesus. Please forgive me and help me be bolder next time.
ROSEMARY GREEN

SUNDAY 12 APRIL   **MARK 16:1–8**

Awestruck at the tomb

As they entered the tomb, they saw a young man dressed in a white robe sitting on the right side, and they were alarmed. 'Don't be alarmed,' he said. 'You are looking for Jesus the Nazarene, who was crucified. He has risen! He is not here.' (NIV)

Salome explains: This sabbath was awful. Passover is usually a time to rejoice, remembering the escape from slavery in Egypt. This year that seemed meaningless beside the grief and disappointment of Jesus' death; my nephew, our friend, our leader gone. Our hopes shattered.

We had watched to the end while Jesus hung there, dying. Joseph of Arimathea had the clout to ask for his body for burial. We knew that he and Nicodemus didn't have time to finish embalming the body fully, so we bought the extra spices in the evening, when the sabbath was over, ready to get to the tomb at first light. On the way we realised we couldn't roll away the heavy stone blocking the entrance to the tomb. But someone had got there first! The tomb was open, and inside, a young man told us not to be scared. 'Jesus has risen.' What was happening?

I think this young man in white must have been an angel, an angel with even greater news than the one who told my sister Mary that she would give birth to Jesus. This one told us that the tomb was empty because Jesus had risen and is alive!

I was puzzled, scared, awestruck, excited all at the same time! Could it be true? What did it all mean?

[*Rosemary*: I grew up in a traditional Anglican home, familiar with the gospels. I accepted the resurrection as a fact of ancient history. But in my late teens I felt there must be something more alive than I had yet found in my Christianity. One particular sermon showed me that Jesus' death was vital for me, the supposed 'goody-goody'. And his resurrection meant that he was alive to be my friend. Decades later that is still the mainspring of my life, but my wonder and excitement need to be renewed daily.]

Lord Jesus, thank you that you died for me. Thank you that you are alive to be my friend. Please renew my wonder and excitement today.

ROSEMARY GREEN

MONDAY 13 APRIL   **MARK 16:9–20**

Exciting news

Later Jesus appeared to the Eleven as they were eating; he rebuked them for their lack of faith and their stubborn refusal to believe those who had seen him after he had risen. He said to them, 'Go into all the world and preach the gospel to all creation.' (NIV)

A commentary by a gospel copyist about 50 years after Holy Week: It's slow work, but exciting. I have finished making a copy of the life and teaching of Jesus, to spread the news further. As I write, it gives me a chance to think more about him and what he means in my life. But when I came to the end I thought, 'The author can't have finished like this, with the women keeping quiet about the most exciting event in history! I think the end of the story has got lost.'

So I have looked carefully at what others have written, and the Spirit has prompted me to add some events that underline the most important tasks for the church. First and foremost is the command to tell the whole world about Jesus.

Some Christians will speak to huge crowds, some to a few, some just to one at a time. 'Go into all the world,' he said. We don't know how big the world is, or how long it will take to reach everyone. But he needs every one of us to do our bit. Not everyone will believe – even Jesus' followers found it hard to believe he was alive. He must have been discouraged when, in the three years he was with his disciples, they were so often slow to understand and to believe. But belief, baptism and declaring that we belong are all essential. And I need to emphasise the power God gives, to enable his servants to heal and to drive out demons. Our God is powerful; we must show that by our changed lives and by the miracles he does.

[*Rosemary*: More than one writer tried to make up for the 'lost' ending of Mark's gospel, but the reading above is the most accepted. It appears the copyist had access to Luke's gospel and probably Matthew and Acts.]

Thank you, Jesus for stimulating me afresh to obey your command to share the good news whenever and wherever I can, and to live in the power of your Spirit.

ROSEMARY GREEN

TUESDAY 14 APRIL MARK 14:31, 66–72

Denial and despair

But Peter insisted emphatically, 'Even if I have to die with you, I will never disown you.' And all the others said the same... [Peter] began to call down curses, and he swore to them, 'I don't know this man you're talking about.' Immediately the cock crowed the second time. (NIV)

Peter grieves: I was so sure of myself! I was going to stand by Jesus, whatever happened, even if the rest of them copied Judas' cowardly desertion. Didn't I use my sword when the rabble assaulted him in the garden? I was going to defend him to the end. So when they dragged him off for interrogation, I stayed as close as I could. I thought the guards would know what was happening, so I sat with them by the brazier. They didn't seem to notice me, till one of the servant girls went past. She looked closely at me and said, 'You were with the Nazarene.' I didn't know where she had seen me, so I denied it: 'He's nothing to do with me!' I was scared, so I walked away. But she was with her friends: 'That man, he's one of Jesus' followers!' I was afraid, so raised my voice: 'You've got it wrong!' Then one of the others said, 'Listen to his accent. He comes from Galilee. He must be one of them.' That alarmed me, and I swore at them: 'You're talking rubbish!'

Then I heard an ominous sound. The cockerel crowed again. I remembered Jesus' warning against my over-confidence. 'Before the cock crows twice, you will deny me three times.' I collapsed in tears. What had I done to my Master? What a miserable coward I am. Wretched, wretched, wretched. How can I be any use to him now? I can hardly bear it.

There's one note of hope – the message the man in white gave the women by the empty tomb. 'Tell his disciples *and Peter*' – that shows I'm still included. But I've let him down so badly, as he knew I would. When he came that evening, I couldn't look him in the eye. I had failed.

Most of us have shared Peter's failure to speak up for Jesus at different times in our lives. But do we share his deep grief and shame for our silence? This can lead to repentance, to deep joy in forgiveness and to renewed witness.

ROSEMARY GREEN

WEDNESDAY 15 APRIL MARK 12:28–34

Love is number one

'The most important [commandment],' answered Jesus, 'is this: 'Hear, O Israel: the Lord our God, the Lord is one. Love the Lord your God with all your heart and with all your soul and with all your mind and with all your strength.' The second is this: 'Love your neighbour as yourself.'' (NIV)

A disciple reflects: Last week was momentous. What stands out for me was Jesus' answer to the rabbi who asked him, 'What is the greatest commandment?' Jesus showed us the motivation behind the law: love for God and love for people, not forgetting love for oneself. We have seen his love and commitment to God in his early rising to pray and his desire to please God all the time. We have seen him loving the marginalised and giving all to the crowds. We ourselves have felt his tough love; even when he rebuked us, we knew he wanted the best for us. He said once of himself, 'The Son of Man did not come to be served, but to serve, and to give his life as a ransom for many.' That is what we saw supremely on Friday; his love that served in giving his life. And, as he faced constant opposition, we have seen the security that came from his right love for himself.

That wholehearted love is what he asks of us: to love him with our whole being and to love other people, even the apparently unlovable. And if we love ourselves rightly, we will each know we are worth something. It's an exciting, daunting standard. At the Passover meal, Jesus made clear how these prime commandments are to be lived out. 'If you love me, keep my commandments.' Obedience born of love, not duty. He added his new command, 'As I have loved you, so you must love one another.' I want to live Jesus' life of love.

[*Rosemary*: Forty-seven years ago, I realised how little I knew about loving other people. I read 1 Corinthians 13 and prayed half-heartedly for that love. I feared having to give to other people. Then, in my need, I let friends love me. God's love was planted in me, and I found a new freedom to love Jesus and to love people with God's love.]

Lord, please keep your love fresh in me.

ROSEMARY GREEN

THURSDAY 16 APRIL MARK 12:41–44

Love in action

Calling his disciples to him, Jesus said, 'Truly I tell you, this poor widow has put more into the treasury than all the others. They all gave out of their wealth; but she, out of her poverty, put in everything – all she had to live on.' (NIV)

A disciple reflects: Soon after Jesus had told us about the greatest commandments, to love God and to love people, we saw a beautiful example of that love in action. Jesus deliberately stopped to sit and watch people bringing their offerings for the temple treasury. Many of the rich men made a great show of throwing in their handfuls of coins to make a loud clatter. I remembered how Jesus taught us earlier about the hypocrites whose ostentatious giving reaps their rewards from the plaudits of other people. In fact, he had just been warning us against the religious legal experts who flaunt their importance and their religiosity in front of us all. They don't do any real work; instead, they prey on defenceless women. No rewards for them from our Father in heaven; indeed, Jesus says that heavy punishment awaits them.

Then a lady who looked utterly poverty-stricken walked up quietly and slipped two tiny coins into the offering. Jesus understood how much those coins were worth to her. 'That's all she had to live on.' She gave everything she had. That remarkable, self-denying, lavish generosity is a mark of how much she loves God – with her heart and soul and mind and strength. She puts me to shame. I'm glad Jesus noticed her and drew our attention to her. She wanted to hide but she's the one, not those hypocrites, who deserves to be noticed and applauded. Our Father in heaven knows her devotion. I hope she gets her reward on earth as well as in heaven.

[*Rosemary*: That widow was a challenge to the disciples, and she is a challenge to me, too. I think with shame of the times when I have given less than I might have done to people in deep need, for fear of leaving too little for ourselves.]

Lord, I pray that your Spirit at work in me may enhance my love for you and my sacrificial love for other people.

ROSEMARY GREEN

FRIDAY 17 APRIL   **MARK 13:1–13**

Troubles to come

'You yourselves must watch out. You will be arrested and taken to court. You will be beaten in the synagogues; you will stand before rulers and kings for my sake to tell them the Good News. But before the end comes, the gospel must be preached to all peoples.' (GNT)

Andrew reflects: It was a rare treat for me to be included today with the inner trio, as we sat with Jesus looking across the Kidron valley from the Mount of Olives towards the temple. What he said seemed perplexing at first; then I realised we had combined two questions, which had separate answers. He had warned us, to our astonishment, that the new temple would be utterly destroyed. We had asked him when this would happen, and what warning signs we might see, and he warned us about many false claimants to be the Messiah, about natural disasters, about fighting and turmoil.

What struck me most was all he said about being persecuted. Times are going to be tough. If we stand up for Jesus and all that he means to us, we will be hauled in front of the courts and thrown out of the synagogues. That may mean we will be mocked, or experience unfair trials, even torture. He didn't spell out that we would be in danger of losing our lives but I guess that might happen too. Even families will be divided, some on his side, some against. Will I have the courage to stand up for him? I suppose I cannot be sure until I am tested.

Two things he said really encouraged me. One is that the trials will all help the good news about him to be spread further. The other is his promise that we do not have to worry too much beforehand about how we will cope or what we will say, because the Holy Spirit is going to help us. I don't understand about his Spirit, but if it means that I can share something of Jesus' strength, that will be wonderful.

Much religious persecution in the world is directed against Christians. In our own country, antagonism against our convictions is growing. I pray for the courage to stand against any opposition, verbal or physical, I may meet.

ROSEMARY GREEN

SATURDAY 18 APRIL MARK 13:24–37

Looking towards the end

'At that time people will see the Son of Man coming in clouds with great power and glory. And he will send his angels and gather his elect from the four winds, from the ends of the earth to the ends of the heavens.' (NIV)

Peter thinks of the future: As five of us sat on the Mount of Olives looking towards the magnificent, gilded temple, only recently completed, Jesus warned us that it would be completely destroyed. But I was grabbed most by the last part of what he said. Was he looking towards the culmination of everything on the earth as we know it? And he spoke of himself coming in glory. He came to this earth as a baby in obscurity, almost totally unnoticed. We have known him as a real man, both ordinary and extraordinary. Three of us had the privilege, once, of seeing him wonderfully transfigured. That was only for a moment, to give us a glimpse of his eternal glory.

But one day, he says, he will come in a way that will be unmistakable, unavoidable. He will come in splendour and glory. His attendant angels will gather together the people who are truly his – I suppose to be with him forever. It is almost impossible to grasp. But Jesus said that no one, not even he, knows when that will happen. So we have to be ready for it at any time. I liked his illustration: if the owner of the house goes away, leaving his servants in charge, they don't know when he will return; they have to be alert and ready all the time. If the king was coming to my house, what a to-do there would be getting everything spick and span! Jesus, the greatest King of all, is coming again one day; I must make sure I am expectant and ready.

In 2 Peter 3:11–12, Peter wrote: 'You ought to live holy and godly lives as you look forward to the day of God and speed its coming.' A good question to ask myself: Would I be happy, or ashamed, if Jesus were to come back now?

ROSEMARY GREEN

Elijah and Elisha: faithful messengers

Fiona Barnard writes:

'The nail that sticks up gets hammered down,' states a Japanese proverb. And so we end up in a world where there is a sameness to things. You can have any colour of carpet as long as it is beige. Carrots adorn the supermarket shelves, but they are all straight and equal size. Perhaps it is just me, but I get totally confused with who is in power these days, because the politicians all look and talk the same. Our risk-averse society has diluted us. Mediocrity rules. Yet at the same time, we watch helplessly as things deteriorate around us. Poverty and desperation, fake news and social disintegration don't get resolved, for all the policies and initiatives we throw at them.

Well, in the stories of Elijah and Elisha, we are in for a shake-up. Because these nails stick up and stay up, despite the hammering. In dark years of covenant infidelity championed by the evil Queen Jezebel and King Ahab, Elijah stands out: faithful, loyal, persistent, bold. He declares searing truth to tyrannical power. He takes on the entrenched religious establishment. Then Elisha is trained by Elijah to carry Yahweh's message onward. They both involve themselves in the political and social affairs of the day long before democracy made it normal. They speak of God's tender practical care to the most vulnerable.

Our context today may seem far removed from the hot dusty days of the ninth century BC, but I wonder if our journey with them over the next two weeks may call us to be the Lord's mouth and hands and feet in fresh ways.

Lest we imagine that we could never be that brave and radical, we are given glimpses behind the scenes. We see something of the personal cost of this calling. And for our encouragement, we observe in the relationship between Elijah and Elisha that godly servants are formed, not ready-made. The mentoring of Elisha inspires us to see the enormous contribution of those who are further on in the faith. We do not do God's bidding by ourselves. We were never meant to be lone rangers. Our brothers and sisters in Christ enter the battle with us. So, hold on to your seats and let the word of God be heard!

SUNDAY 19 APRIL **1 KINGS 17:1–6**

'Yahweh is God'

Now Elijah, who was from Tishbe in Gilead, told King Ahab, 'As surely as the Lord, the God of Israel, lives – the God I serve – there will be no dew or rain during the next few years until I give the word!' (NLT)

If you, like me, live in a 'green and pleasant land', lack of rain is seldom a serious concern. The lawn may go a bit brown in the summer, but water still gushes out of the tap. Failing that, the supermarket can sell you the bottled stuff. You will be able to select from an abundance of potatoes and leeks, imported oranges and grapes. We are the fortunate ones in a world where vast continents are at the mercy of extreme climate change. Flash floods and droughts have a direct bearing on the ability of millions to provide food on the table for their families.

In a land dependent on winter rain and summer dew for year-round moisture, ancient farming communities knew they had no control over the elements.

King Ahab, urged by his wife Jezebel, had turned his back on the creator God of earth and sky in favour of the Canaanite fertility gods. In what feels like a cosmic battle, Elijah brings the challenge of Yahweh in a language Ahab will understand: God demonstrates his sovereignty in the giving or withdrawal of rain. He is the one who can provide for his people.

We cannot underestimate the courage of Elijah. He brings unwelcome news to an evil, despotic ruler. He contests the reign of Baal. How does he do it? The key is in his name, which means 'Yahweh is God'. His opening words literally translate, 'The God before whom I have stood.' For me, this is an evocative image of an ever-attentive subject and confidant, ready to respond to the word and will of the Master. The strength to make a difference in our world comes from that intimacy with Christ. The passion to speak God's saving truths derives from a listening, devoted heart.

As we start this series, ask God for a hearing heart and a deeper concern for his broken world.

FIONA BARNARD

MONDAY 20 APRIL 1 KINGS 17:7–16

Living by faith

[The widow at Zarephath] said… 'I was just gathering a few sticks to cook this last meal, and then my son and I will die.' But Elijah said to her, 'Don't be afraid!… Make a little bread for me first. Then use what's left to prepare a meal for yourself and your son.' (NLT)

God is full of surprises. Following him leads to unexpected adventures. He called Elijah to speak to his people Israel, but here sends him to Zarephath, a village outside the land. He commissioned him to challenge the apostasy of King Ahab, but redirects him to find a particular pagan woman. He has prepared this defenceless widow on the brink of starvation to feed him. You could not make it up.

That is the point. Our God works in astonishing ways. While his covenant people bargain for rain from the god Baal, the creator is not manipulated. Through Elijah, he calls for risky faith, asking a hopeless victim of drought and famine for water and bread. When she gives the last of her food to Elijah, God responds to her sacrifice with a miracle that saves her family's life. Faithful to his promise, God tops up her containers of flour and oil until the rains and crops return. In the heart of a Baal-worshipping land, both prophet and pagan hostess feed on Yahweh's food and astounding grace.

'Living by faith' was what we used to call doing things for God without enough money for it. I went to Bible College with no grant and little savings. My faith was small, and almost snuffed out as I underwent extreme spiritual testing. I failed at 'living by faith' in many ways. Yet by graduation, I had more money in my bank account than when I started. God's generous provision still flummoxes me whenever I recall it. I don't understand why he did it for me. In the pecking order of social and religious significance, the widow was on the bottom rung. So was I. God chooses the least on whom to pour his outrageous kindness. We do indeed live by faith.

Bring to God any you know who are struggling to afford the basic necessities of life.

FIONA BARNARD

TUESDAY 21 APRIL   **1 KINGS 17:17–24**

Breathing life

Elijah cried out to the Lord, 'O Lord my God, why have you brought tragedy to this widow who has opened her home to me, causing her son to die?… My God, please let this child's life return to him.' The Lord heard Elijah's prayer, and the life of the child returned. (NLT)

'Oh Lord, why?' is a prayer of intense anguish, profound bewilderment, audacious faith. It is the outraged shriek of pain struggling to make sense of heartbreak and calamity. It is the cry that howls, 'It is not *fair*!'

Elijah is distraught at the death of the widow's child. This son, as her only male offspring, was her passport to a more hopeful future, but his life has been cut short. How could her hospitality be rewarded by tragedy? Might she interpret her loss as revenge from the gods for sheltering Yahweh's prophet?

Elijah, feeling the depths of grief, hammers on heaven's doors and intercedes for his friend. Lying on the child's lifeless body, he acts out his prayer, 'May this lifeless body be like mine, full of life.' The child breathes again. The family reunion convinces an ecstatic mother that Elijah's God is real and that he speaks through his prophet. This domestic moment also has a wider significance in God's salvation history as non-Jews witness the power of Yahweh.

Today, I was at a funeral. I am sure the family will have been asking, 'Oh Lord, why?' I can imagine that they would love for a prophet or doctor to restore their loved one. It hasn't happened. Sorrow is real. But today, the certain hope of the resurrection was tangible. Amid the tears was a sense that for those in Christ, this is not the end. Mourning is appropriate when we say 'goodbye', but we are really saying, 'See you later.' This is a message that a world reeling with loss needs to hear. The assurance of life is not just an empty platitude for a card of condolence, not just wishful thinking to comfort the bereaved. It is the promise of Jesus, who himself passed from death to new life.

Bring to God those who are struggling with personal loss.

FIONA BARNARD

WEDNESDAY 22 APRIL 1 KINGS 18:16–40

Crunch time

[Elijah] said, 'How much longer will you waver, hobbling between two opinions? If the Lord is God, follow him! But if Baal is God, then follow him!'… [He] prayed, 'O Lord, God of Abraham, Isaac, and Jacob, prove today that you are God in Israel and that I am your servant.' (NLT)

'Who is she praying to?' I asked a Japanese friend when she took me to a temple. 'The gods,' she replied. 'What are the gods like?' Her answer was echoed by a number of people in my travels around the Far East: 'We don't know.' There, I observed a very different understanding of God. Focusing on ritual and practice rather than doctrine and story, religious notions intermingle freely. The 'gods' are spiritual forces believed to affect individuals for good or ill in relationships, business, health and travel. They have to be appeased, with uncertain, even capricious, results.

Elijah's rallying cry to the people of Israel brooks no compromise. He challenges them to make a decision one way or another. They are limping unsteadily, one leg for Baal, the other for Yahweh. Now it is crunch time. Will they pursue the local Canaanite fertility gods or be faithful to Yahweh? Who is real? Which is able to provide for them: the impersonal manifestations of Baal or the personal covenant God of their ancestors Abraham, Isaac and Jacob?

On a mountaintop, an epic power encounter is enacted for all to witness. The day-long ranting and self-mutilation of 450 Baal prophets proves futile. The prayer of Elijah alone brings fire from heaven, consuming the soaking wet sacrifice, along with the water, wood and stones. The evidence is incontestable: 'The Lord – he is God!' shout the people in response. Yahweh is present. He is sovereign over nature.

Recently, we heard from a Chinese friend: 'I have decided to identify myself as a Christian.' Having watched and listened, she is convinced. She has made a decision. Her parents may be outraged but when it comes to following Jesus, there can be no negotiation. He calls for our exclusive devotion.

Are there ways in which you are compromising your loyalty to Christ?

FIONA BARNARD

THURSDAY 23 APRIL 1 KINGS 19:1–18

Burnout and restoration

Elijah was afraid and fled for his life… [He] prayed that he might die. 'I have had enough, Lord,' he said. 'Take my life…' As he was sleeping, an angel touched him and told him, 'Get up and eat!' He looked around and there beside his head was some bread baked on hot stones and a jar of water! (NLT)

There is a cost to following the Lord wholeheartedly. You give more time when you have lots to do already. You offer hospitality to guests who are reluctant to leave. You pop in on an elderly neighbour, accept another year on a committee, put the chairs away when everyone has gone home. You pray and agonise over a project which fails. Sometimes it feels as though all the air has been sucked out of you. You are physically and emotionally and spiritually crushed.

Elijah is suicidal. Like a hero in an epic, he has taken on the false Canaanite gods, the wicked Queen Jezebel and King Ahab, the 450 false prophets. Standing tall, this solitary figure has challenged the forces of evil with the word of God. He has waged war, and now, although he has won, he is terribly wounded. These are honourable battle scars, but he is exhausted. He is famished and fearful. He feels alone. Jezebel's threat to kill him is the last straw. There is something poignantly beautiful about the way God deals with Elijah. He lets him sleep. He sends an angel who wakes him gently with warm bread and cool water. He takes him away from the action. He lets him walk for several weeks. When Elijah is still, he encourages him to pour out his anguish. He assures him he is not alone but part of a team. He whispers his care and gives him a plan of action.

Soldiering on for a time may be right, but depression, ill health and a martyr spirit can be the consequences if we do not recharge. Food and sleep, exercise and music, holidays and retreats are all gifts whereby we are renewed, where we meet God afresh and hear his call again.

'He makes me lie down in green pastures… He refreshes my soul' (Psalm 23:2–3, NIV). Let him do it.

FIONA BARNARD

FRIDAY 24 APRIL 　　　　　　　　　　　　　　　**1 KINGS 19:19–21**

The mentoring cloak

Elijah went and found Elisha… ploughing a field… Elijah went over to him and threw his cloak across his shoulders and then walked away. Elisha left the oxen standing there, ran after Elijah, and said to him, 'First let me go and kiss my father and mother good-bye, and then I will go with you!' (NLT)

Mary was the first person to welcome me for meals when I went to university. She regaled me with tales about the town and the characters in the church so I felt I belonged. She wrote regularly when I spent a summer in India and gave me opportunities to speak about my experience when I returned. She supported my developing service in the church through regular prayer and blunt advice. I watched her become the first female deacon my church ordained. I noticed the way she led groups and participated in local and global mission. I heard her voice opinions and dreams and solutions. Now 20 years later, I was at her deathbed, wondering what I could say. Before I knew it, I heard myself speak: 'You have been Elijah to my Elisha.' That day I understood her cloak had been put across my shoulders despite all my inadequacies and fears.

Part of Elijah's restoration after his burnout is to recognise he is not alone. He is commissioned to mentor Elisha as his successor. Throwing his prophetic cloak over Elisha's shoulders is a summons to be a disciple. He walks away to let Elisha consider. This call will cost everything: time with family, wealth and social status. Yet God has prepared Elisha's heart. He slaughters his oxen, builds a fire with the plough and says goodbye to his parents. There is no turning back. The feast with his neighbours is a celebration, a recognition of his ordination.

We cannot overestimate the value of learning from those further on in faith. These prayerful relationships, whether as formal or informal mentoring, are often low-key. Usually they are best done by people too humble to imagine they have anything to offer. And yet for those with a teachable spirit, they are life-changing.

Think of someone who had a significant impact on your Christian life and thank God for them. Who is God calling you to encourage now?

FIONA BARNARD

SATURDAY 25 APRIL **1 KINGS 21**

Speaking truth to power

The Lord said to Elijah, 'Go down to meet King Ahab of Israel, who rules in Samaria. He will be at Naboth's vineyard in Jezreel, claiming it for himself. Give him this message: "This is what the Lord says: Wasn't it enough that you killed Naboth? Must you rob him, too?"' (NLT)

It is costly to speak truth to power. Despots don't like it. Cocooned in a world of entitlement, egos demand pampering, not challenge. Those who question or refuse a tyrant's will are either courageous or crazy. The prisons and graves throughout history bear witness.

On the surface, Ahab's business proposition is fair. He offers Naboth money for his vineyard, which neighbours his palace, with the intention of turning it into a vegetable patch. When the expected positive response is not forthcoming, he retreats to bed in a sulk. His wife Jezebel is outraged: 'You are king, for goodness sake! I'll make that man pay for his non-compliance.' Running roughshod over justice and truth, she has Naboth killed on trumped-up charges of blasphemy and confiscates his property. The incident may well have been overlooked in a reign where evil is the norm. But God notices. He cares about family livelihood. His loving provision through the laws on land allocation has been cruelly violated. Naboth has paid with his life for loyalty to God's covenant. So Elijah is given the fearsome task of calling Ahab and Jezebel to account. He announces Yahweh's punishment on their greed and murder.

In a world where misuse of power in many disguises is endemic, God's people are called to speak out on behalf of the oppressed. Whether it is cronyism or bullying in the staff room, forced marriages or economic sleaze, flagrant seizure of assets or slaughter in distant lands, our love of God must surely summon us to action. May God grant us wisdom and compassion and righteous anger to act ourselves, and to pray for and support all those in the battle for fairness and human dignity.

'What does the Lord require of you but to do justice, and to love kindness, and to walk humbly with your God?' (Micah 6:8, NRSV).

FIONA BARNARD

SUNDAY 26 APRIL   **2 KINGS 2:1–18**

Legacy

As they were walking along and talking, suddenly a chariot of fire appeared, drawn by horses of fire. It drove between the two men, separating them, and Elijah was carried by a whirlwind into heaven. Elisha saw it and cried out, 'My father! My father! I see the chariots and charioteers of Israel!' (NLT)

There were many tearful farewells when our much-loved minister retired and moved away. So many people were grateful for his warm pastoral care in moments of crisis and loss, spiritual awakening and doubt. We relished his sensitive handling of scripture and the way he conducted services and meetings. We dreaded his leaving. However, a few months later, as I look round our congregation, I see fruit from his careful work of preparing us. Many have stepped up to new roles and responsibilities during this time of pastoral vacancy. Twenty people have asked to become members. The work with young people and migrants and the elderly continues. In his absence, we are heartened by the legacy he has left behind.

Elijah's departure is anticipated with foreboding. He has been a colossal figure in the social, political and religious life of Israel. He has been God's messenger, involved in national affairs, forming strategy for war and diplomacy, providing for the vulnerable, holding kings to account and reminding the people of their covenant with God. What will happen when he goes? Elisha, his disciple, cannot bear the thought.

While we may not understand how he is whirled up to heaven, Elijah's legacy stretches across the millennia. Staggeringly, he appears with Moses on the mount of transfiguration to talk with Jesus about his death. I wonder what he says. Might Elijah have encouraged Jesus at a time of crucial, yet painful decision-making? Imagine it: 'You are doing what I never could. Your coming is bringing people to the Father. This is how they will have their lives turned around to face God! This is how the hungry will be fed, the oppressed set free, the dead raised. Your departure through death and resurrection is where history has been leading. This is it. Praise God!'

What legacy is benefitting you? What legacy will you leave behind?

                                                                    FIONA BARNARD

MONDAY 27 APRIL 2 KINGS 2:1–18

The Spirit's power

Elijah said to Elisha, 'Tell me what I can do for you before I am taken away.' And Elisha replied, 'Please let me inherit a double share of your spirit and become your successor'… Elijah replied, 'If you see me when I am taken from you, then you will get your request.' (NLT)

Every Friday I light a candle before the international students' Bible study meets in my house. It serves as a prayer for this holy task. I feel so inadequate. What will make a difference so I can help people to grow in faith? What makes the difference for any of us, parent, leader, mentor, friend, disciple?

Elisha does not want to let go of Elijah. He has accompanied the prophet, watched and listened to him. He loves him as a father. Every mention of Elijah being 'taken away' makes his stomach lurch. Finally, Elijah asks a question which reveals Elisha's heart: 'What can I do for you?' The bereft mentee responds, 'If you really must leave, my father, and if I am to become your successor, please let me be like you, like a first-born son. I desperately need whatever it is that has formed and sustained you.' Then he sees the fiery chariots which separate him and Elijah: the chariots denoting power, the fire manifesting the glory of God's presence. The wind that carries Elijah away comes from the breath of God. The Spirit of God, presence of God in his servant: that is what will make the difference. As Elisha returns to a new phase of ministry, he replicates Elijah's miracle, separating the waters of the river, much like Moses of old. His commissioning is confirmed by others.

In our service for Christ, we face times of bewilderment and fear. Sometimes we are stumped by situations or people who create seemingly impassable obstacles. We cry, 'Lord, I cannot do this. It is too much for me!' Our empty-handedness enables us to reach out to God afresh. He comes to us. He reminds us that the work is his: his Spirit is active even amid our desolation.

If God were to ask you, 'What can I do for you?', how would you respond?

FIONA BARNARD

TUESDAY 28 APRIL 2 KINGS 5:1–19

Pointing to the God of the whole world

Naaman went down to the Jordan River and dipped himself seven times, as the man of God had instructed him… Naaman said, 'Now I know that there is no God in all the world except in Israel. So please accept a gift from your servant'… Elisha replied… 'I will not accept any gifts.' (NLT)

'What is the religion in Sri Lanka? China? Jamaica?' I am occasionally asked. It is as though God is provincial and needs a passport to get out of his allotted territory. Sometimes international students with whom I work suddenly appear at church during exams or ask for baptism without any knowledge of Christianity. They want to keep in with the 'local' god. We do explore motivation, but this sense of need can be a wonderful opportunity to introduce them to Jesus.

In our readings, we might be tempted to imagine that Yahweh is Israel's. But this story stops us short. Here we have a proclamation of Yahweh as the only God of the whole world. It is declared not by a priest or a prophet, but by a pagan non-Israelite: a high-ranking army commander desperate enough to abandon all his conditions and presuppositions to be cured of leprosy. Yahweh has healed him. Simply. Beautifully. Not through the tricks of a wonderworker nor the expertise of a professional; not through payment of money nor complicated self-help. This God cannot be bought or manipulated. This God has cleansed his diseased skin out of sheer grace, through his humble obedience to Elisha's instruction. There is no other God like him. Naaman returns to Syria a new person, inside and out.

Christians can be confident that Jesus shines supremely bright above other religious claims in our multicultural society. We who know his salvation and healing have good news to share with the guilty and troubled. We who experience his care when we are despairing can point to him. We who recognise his grace reaching across borders of race and social position can worship him and lift him high as God of the whole earth.

How can you lift Jesus high today?

FIONA BARNARD

WEDNESDAY 29 APRIL 2 KINGS 5:20–27

The discipline of love

[Gehazi] said to himself, 'My master should not have let this Aramean get away without accepting any of his gifts. As surely as the Lord lives, I will chase after him and get something from him'… Then he went and hid the gifts inside the house. (NLT)

I have a resident critic inside me who gives a running commentary on most of what I do and deems it rubbish. The meal, the conversation, the lesson are inevitably useless. This familiar inner voice is unreliable background mumbling. What I really need is someone who cares enough about me to give honest feedback both on my performance and my character. I relish the encouraging card or call pinpointing a specific positive. But I also value the challenge of a kind conversation when I am out of line, especially if it illustrates an aspect of my personality which the Spirit wants to change.

Gehazi is called Elisha's servant. Was he simply a person who supported the prophet in meals and travel, or was there an aspect of mentoring for future ministry, as Elijah had done for Elisha? Either way, his greed in wanting some of Naaman's gifts is outrageous. This is compounded by lies when he tells Naaman that Elisha needs provisions for unexpected visitors, and deceit when Elisha questions him. Hiding his ill-gotten gains reveals a guilty heart which has not understood the God of grace. As someone in a privileged position, close to the man of God, his action has wider consequences: he has given a false impression to Naaman about God's ways. And so Elisha confronts him and he is punished. His diseased skin will always remind him not to dishonour the Lord's holy reputation.

This tantalising glimpse into Elisha's dealing with Gehazi leaves us with many questions. Yet as I have thought about it, these words in Hebrews come to mind: 'The Lord disciplines those he loves' (12:6). Divine correction, even through human beings, demonstrates a caring commitment to our spiritual growth.

'God's discipline is always good for us, so that we might share in his holiness' (Hebrews 12:10). Pray for grace to respond to the Spirit's loving work in your life.

FIONA BARNARD

THURSDAY 30 APRIL 2 KINGS 8:1–6

God's CV

The king had just said, 'Tell me some stories about the great things Elisha has done.' And Gehazi was telling the king about the time Elisha had brought a boy back to life. At that very moment, the mother of the boy walked in to make her appeal to the king about her house and land. (NLT)

CVs are strange documents. There's an art to listing qualifications, experience and achievements so that sometimes the most incompetent can appear as experts. What you cannot control are the stories told about you. They cast a whole different light on you and your achievements.

These last two weeks have given us a varied collection of narratives about God's prophets. We have watched Elijah in his brave but bruising battles against Baalism. We have followed his mentoring of Elisha, as he speaks God's word and cares for the vulnerable. We have seen Elisha developing a wonder-working ministry. These would have been the stories Gehazi was relating to the king: Elisha dividing the river Jordan, purifying poisoned water for a school of prophets, providing bread for a hundred people, enabling a valuable axe head to be retrieved by making it float in a river, multiplying oil for a desperate widow. Take time to read them. Most impressive is a miracle similar to one Elijah performed: the raising of a much-loved only child back to life. The king might have been shaking his head in disbelief until 'by chance' the mother herself appears with her son to confirm everything.

The CV God's Spirit writes for you is very different from the one you use to secure a job. You may feel overwhelmed and uncertain whether you can live up to your calling. But by God's grace, your attitudes and choices serve as inspiration and guidance to others in ways you could never imagine. And one day, whether you disappear in a whirlwind to heaven like Elijah (unlikely) or are buried in the earth like Elisha (probably), mourners at your funeral may hear the testimonies of colleagues and neighbours, family and friends who have seen God's Spirit at work in you and give glory to him.

What has impressed you about the lives of Elijah and Elisha?

FIONA BARNARD

Day by Day with God is on Instagram!

Follow us for a daily quote from *Day by Day with God*,
to help you meet with God in the everyday.

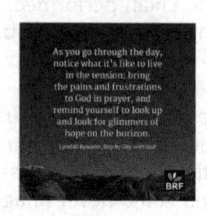

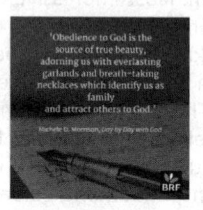

Follow us: @daybydaywithgod

Help us raise God-connected children and teens through a gift in your will

Aged twelve, Jesus went with his family to Jerusalem to celebrate the Feast of Passover. After the festival, the family began their journey home, but Jesus was not among them. He stayed behind 'in the temple courts, sitting among the teachers, listening to them and asking them questions' (Luke 2:46, NIV).

It's a picture that may sound familiar to some parents. Perhaps you can remember a time when you were trying to get your kids ready for school, a family meal or another engagement. There was much to do and time was slipping away, but all your kids wanted to do was ask questions about anything and everything.

As a parent, you often want to encourage your children to ask questions, spiritual or otherwise, so that they can learn and discover new things. But life must go on and those shoe laces won't tie themselves! It's a tricky predicament.

Our **Parenting for Faith** team understands this dichotomy. They aim to equip parents and carers to confidently parent for faith in the midst of the mundane: when ferrying the children back and forth, sitting on the bathroom floor potty-training toddlers or waving kids off on their first day of secondary school.

Through their website, an eight-session course and numerous events and training opportunities, the Parenting for Faith team are helping Christian parents raise God-connected children and teens. They're helping to raise a new generation that can bring God's love to a world in need.

Could you help this work continue by leaving a gift in your will? Even a small amount can help make a lasting difference in the lives of parents and children.

For further information about making a gift to BRF in your will, please visit brf.org.uk/lastingdifference, contact us at **+44 (0)1865 319700** or email giving@brf.org.uk.

Whatever you can do or give, we thank you for your support.

> Pray. Give. Get involved.
> **brf.org.uk**

At this time of Lent, David Walker explores different aspects of human belonging through the medium of scripture and story in order to help us recognise the different ways in which we are God's beloved. And as we recognise ourselves and our own lives in the narrative of God's engagement with humanity and his creation, he gently challenges us to engage for God's sake with God's world.

You Are Mine
Daily Bible readings from Ash Wednesday to Easter Day
David Walker
978 0 85746 758 4 £8.99
brfonline.org.uk

The Rule of St Benedict has much to say about faith, work and daily living. In a time when many are seeking space, silence and spiritual depth, the Rule retains relevance in a world where change is often feared, stability can be elusive and busyness interferes with listening to God. *Life with St Benedict* provides daily reflections on the Rule as an aid to enabling personal spiritual growth and prayer.

Life with St Benedict
The Rule reimagined for everyday living
Richard Frost
978 0 85746 813 0 £9.99
brfonline.org.uk

To order

Online: **brfonline.org.uk**
Telephone: +44 (0)1865 319700
Mon–Fri 9.15–17.30

Delivery times within the UK are normally 15 working days. Prices are correct at the time of going to press but may change without prior notice.

BRF

Title	Price	Qty	Total
Really Useful Guides: Genesis 1—11	£5.99		
BRF Lent book: You Are Mine	£8.99		
Life with St Benedict	£9.99		
Day by Day with God (Jan–Apr 2020) – single copy	£4.60		
Day by Day with God (May–Aug 2020) – single copy	£4.70		

POSTAGE AND PACKING CHARGES			
Order value	UK	Europe	Rest of world
Under £7.00	£2.00	Available on request	Available on request
£7.00–£29.99	£3.00		
£30.00 and over	FREE		

Total value of books	
Postage and packing	
Total for this order	

Please complete in BLOCK CAPITALS

Title _____ First name/initials _____ Surname _____

Address _____

_____ Postcode _____

Acc. No. _____ Telephone _____

Email _____

Method of payment

☐ Cheque (made payable to BRF)   ☐ MasterCard / Visa credit / Visa debit

Card no. ☐☐☐☐ ☐☐☐☐ ☐☐☐☐ ☐☐☐☐

Expires end [M M] [Y Y]   Security code* ☐☐☐   Last 3 digits on the reverse of the card

Signature* _____ Date _____ / _____ / _____

*ESSENTIAL IN ORDER TO PROCESS YOUR ORDER

Please return this form to:
BRF, 15 The Chambers, Vineyard, Abingdon OX14 3FE | **enquiries@brf.org.uk**
To read our terms and find out about cancelling your order, please visit **brfonline.org.uk/terms**.

The Bible Reading Fellowship (BRF) is a Registered Charity (233280)

DBDWG0120

SUBSCRIPTION INFORMATION

Each issue of *Day by Day with God* is available from Christian bookshops everywhere. Copies may also be available through your church book agent or from the person who distributes Bible reading notes in your church.

Alternatively you may obtain *Day by Day with God* on subscription direct from the publishers. There are two kinds of subscription:

Individual subscriptions
covering 3 issues for 4 copies or less, payable in advance (including postage & packing).

To order, please complete the details on page 144 and return with the appropriate payment to: BRF, 15 The Chambers, Vineyard, Abingdon OX14 3FE

You can also use the form on page 144 to order a gift subscription for a friend.

Group subscriptions
covering 3 issues for 5 copies or more, sent to one UK address (post free).

Please note that the annual billing period for group subscriptions runs from 1 May to 30 April.

To order, please complete the details on page 143 and return with the appropriate payment to: BRF, 15 The Chambers, Vineyard, Abingdon OX14 3FE

You will receive an invoice with the first issue of notes.

All our Bible reading notes can be ordered online by visiting **brfonline.org.uk/collections/subscriptions**

Day by Day with God is also available as an app for Android, iPhone and iPad
brfonline.org.uk/collections/apps

All subscription enquiries should be directed to:
BRF, 15 The Chambers, Vineyard, Abingdon OX14 3FE
+44 (0)1865 319700 | **enquiries@brf.org.uk**

DAY BY DAY WITH GOD GROUP SUBSCRIPTION FORM

All our Bible reading notes can be ordered online by visiting
brfonline.org.uk/collections/subscriptions

The group subscription rate for *Day by Day with God* will be £14.10 per person until April 2021.

☐ I would like to take out a group subscription for .... (quantity) copies.

☐ Please start my order with the May 2020 / September 2020 / January 2021* issue. I would like to pay annually/receive an invoice* with each edition of the notes. (*delete as appropriate)

Please do not send any money with your order. Send your order to BRF and we will send you an invoice. The group subscription year is from 1 May to 30 April. If you start subscribing in the middle of a subscription year we will invoice you for the remaining number of issues left in that year.

Name and address of the person organising the group subscription:

Title .... First name/initials .... Surname ....

Address..

.... Postcode ....

Telephone .... Email ....

Church..

Name of Minister ....

Name and address of the person paying the invoice if the invoice needs to be sent directly to them:

Title .... First name/initials .... Surname ....

Address..

.... Postcode ....

Telephone .... Email ....

Please return this form to:
BRF, 15 The Chambers, Vineyard, Abingdon OX14 3FE | **enquiries@brf.org.uk**

To read our terms and find out about cancelling your order,
please visit **brfonline.org.uk/terms**.

The Bible Reading Fellowship is a Registered Charity (233280)

DAY BY DAY WITH GOD INDIVIDUAL/GIFT SUBSCRIPTION FORM

To order online, please visit **brfonline.org.uk/collections/subscriptions**

☐ I would like to give a gift subscription (please provide both names and addresses)
☐ I would like to take out a subscription myself (complete your name and address details only once)

Title _____ First name/initials _____ Surname _____

Address _____

_____ Postcode _____

Telephone _____ Email _____

Gift subscription name _____

Gift subscription address _____

_____ Postcode _____

Gift subscription (20 words max. or include your own gift card):

_____

_____

Please send *Day by Day with God* beginning with the May 2020 / September 2020 / January 2021 issue (*delete as appropriate*):

(*please tick box*)	UK	Europe	Rest of world
1-year subscription	☐ £17.85	☐ £25.80	☐ £29.70
2-year subscription	☐ £33.90	N/A	N/A

Total enclosed £ _____ (cheques should be made payable to 'BRF')

Please charge my MasterCard / Visa credit / Visa debit with £ _____

Card no. ☐☐☐☐ ☐☐☐☐ ☐☐☐☐ ☐☐☐☐

Expires end ☐M☐M ☐Y☐Y Security code* ☐☐ Last 3 digits on the reverse of the card

Signature* _____ Date _____/_____/_____
*ESSENTIAL IN ORDER TO PROCESS YOUR ORDER

Please return this form to:
BRF, 15 The Chambers, Vineyard, Abingdon OX14 3FE | **enquiries@brf.org.uk**

To read our terms and find out about cancelling your order,
please visit **brfonline.org.uk/terms**. The Bible Reading Fellowship is a Registered Charity (233280)

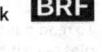